ON ENGLISH PROSE

THE ALEXANDER LECTURESHIP

The Alexander Lectureship was founded in honour of Professor W. J. Alexander, who held the Chair of English at University College, University of Toronto, from 1889 to 1926. Each year the Lectureship brings to the University a distinguished scholar or critic to give a course of lectures on a subject related to English Literature.

ON ENGLISH PROSE

By *James Sutherland*

UNIVERSITY OF TORONTO PRESS

THE ALEXANDER LECTURES

(*Unless otherwise indicated the lectures have been published by the University of Toronto Press*)

1929–30   L. F. CAZAMIAN: "Parallelism in the Recent Development of English and French Literature." Included in the author's *Criticism in the Making* (Macmillan, 1929)

1930–31   H. W. GARROD: *The Study of Poetry* (Clarendon, 1936)

1931–32   IRVING BABBITT: "Wordsworth and Modern Poetry." Included as "The Primitivism of Wordsworth" in the author's *On Being Creative* (Houghton, 1932)

1932–33   W. A. CRAIGIE: *The Northern Element in English Literature* (1933)

1933–34   H. J. C. GRIERSON: "Sir Walter Scott." Included in *Sir Walter Scott, Bart.* (Constable, 1938)

1934–35   G. G. SEDGEWICK: *Of Irony, Especially in Drama* (1934, 1948)

1935–36   E. E. STOLL: *Shakespeare's Young Lovers* (Oxford, 1937)

1936–37   F. B. SNYDER: *Robert Burns, His Personality, His Reputation, and His Art* (1936)

1937–38   D. NICHOL SMITH: *Some Observations on Eighteenth-Century Poetry* (1937)

1938–39   CARLETON W. STANLEY: *Matthew Arnold* (1938)

1939–40   J. DOUGLAS N. BUSH: *The Renaissance and English Humanism* (1939, 1957)

1940–41   No lectures given

1941–42   H. J. DAVIS: *Stella, a Gentlewoman of the Eighteenth Century* (Macmillan, 1942)

1942–43   H. GRANVILLE-BARKER: "Coriolanus." Included in the author's *Prefaces to Shakespeare*, Vol. II (Princeton, 1947)

1943–44   F. P. WILSON: *Elizabethan and Jacobean* (Clarendon, 1945)

1944–45   F. O. MATTHIESSEN: *Henry James, the Major Phase* (Oxford, 1944)

1945–46   S. C. CHEW: *The Virtues Reconciled, an Iconographical Study* (1947)

1946–47   MARJORIE HOPE NICOLSON: *Voyages to the Moon* (Macmillan, 1948)

1947–48   G. B. HARRISON: "Shakespearean Tragedy." Included in the author's *Shakespeare's Tragedies* (Routledge and Kegan Paul, 1951)

1948–49   E. M. W. TILLYARD: *Shakespeare's Problem Plays* (1949)

1949–50   E. K. BROWN: *Rhythm in the Novel* (1950, 1957)

1950–51   MALCOLM W. WALLACE: *English Character and the English Literary Tradition* (1952)

1951–52   R. S. CRANE: *The Languages of Criticism and the Structure of Poetry* (1953, 1957)

1952–53   No lectures given

1953–54   F. M. SALTER: *Mediaeval Drama in Chester* (1955)

1954–55   ALFRED HARBAGE: *Theatre for Shakespeare* (1955)

1955–56   LEON EDEL: *Literary Biography* (1957)

1956–57   JAMES SUTHERLAND: *On English Prose* (1957)

PREFACE

WHEN I WAS HONOURED by an invitation to deliver the Alexander Lectures in 1956, I announced, after due deliberation, that I would lecture on "English Prose." As the months passed, and the day drew near when I was to meet my audience in Toronto, I became more and more alarmed at what I had done, or what, at least, it must appear that I meant to do. To announce that I was going to deal with such a subject as English prose in four lectures now seemed to me likely to strike my audience as a piece of effrontery: I might as well have advertised four lectures on English History or English Poetry. Similar misgivings must have crossed the mind of Professor A. S. P. Woodhouse, for when I arrived at Toronto I found that he had silently emended the title I had sent him from "English Prose" to "On English Prose." This simple alteration expressed so satisfactorily all that I had ever modestly intended to do—to say something about English prose, and the different ways in which it has been written at different periods—that I can only record my gratitude for his timely and intelligent intervention. Although I have advanced in successive lectures from the fourteenth century to the present day, it will be seen that I have made no attempt to write even a brief history of English prose, but have confined my attention to what seemed to me the most important developments, or those about which I thought I had something to say. In the third lecture I have borrowed a few sentences from my essay on "Some Aspects of Eighteenth-Century Prose," which appeared in *Essays on the Eighteenth Century Presented to David Nichol Smith* (1945); and a few more made their first appearance in a paper on "Restoration

Prose," delivered at the William Andrews Clark Memorial Library Seminar, on 14 July, 1956, and subsequently published, along with a paper by Professor Ian Watt, in a pamphlet called *Restoration and Augustan Prose* (1957).

Some of the reading and a good deal of the thinking for these lectures were done during a delightful summer which I had the privilege of spending at the Huntington Library, where I received much kindness and assistance. In preparing them for publication I have added something to all four lectures, but they remain substantially as they were delivered. Of my debts to the work of various scholars I am most fully conscious of those to Professor Morris W. Croll, whose various essays on the prose of the sixteenth and seventeenth centuries are landmarks in the historical study of English prose style; but I have also made use of Professor George Williamson's *The Senecan Amble*, and of the work of Professor R. F. Jones, especially *The Triumph of the English Language*. Professor Woodhouse not only provided me with the right title for my lectures, but he and his colleagues made my visit to Toronto an even greater pleasure than I had expected it to be. In conclusion, I have to thank Professor William Matthews and Professor George Kane for their advice on the first lecture, where I occasionally trespass on territory that lies outside my normal range; and I must express my gratitude to my own colleague, Mr. Charles Peake, who kindly read the manuscript with a care worthy of a better text, and made some valuable suggestions.

J. S.

University College, London
July, 1957

CONTENTS

ON ENGLISH PROSE

I. THE PROBLEM OF PROSE

IN THE HISTORY OF LITERATURE and the history of
individual nations, the development of prose is nearly always
slower and more uncertain than that of poetry. When we go
back to the obscure beginnings of any national literature, what
we usually come upon is some kind of poetry; but we may have
to wait several centuries before we get prose, and even a longer
time before we find it fully articulate, and perhaps longer
still before we meet with prose that it is a pleasure to read. It is
the poets who celebrate the famous deeds of heroes and lament
their misfortunes, who praise the gods, who dignify men's
various activities, who sing of birth, love, and death. All this
they do in verse, which has a special kind of prestige, and even
magic, not usually associated with prose. It is true that those
early bards sometimes used verse to express what, to our more
sophisticated minds, might have been better said in prose; but
not to write in verse would have been, as Abhorson remarked
of a different craft, "to discredit their mystery." When prose
begins to make its first tentative appearance, it is usually in the
form of charters, deeds, proclamations, and practical discourses
of one sort or another; and though from the first it may be well
or badly written, it is hardly likely to be thought of as literature.

In the primitive age of a national literature, then, the very
prestige of poetry acts as a discouragement to prose. What men
want to listen to is the lilting sound of verse rather than the more
pedestrian and unemphatic rhythms of prose. Long after this
primitive stage has passed, we have still to reckon, as W. P. Ker
reminded us, with

the natural antipathy of the natural man to listen to any continuous story except in verse. The dismal multitude of versified encyclopaedias, the rhyming text-books of science, history, and morality, are there to witness of the reluctance with which prose was accepted to do the ordinary prose drudgery.[1]

In accounting for the comparatively slow development of prose we must remember that if we go far enough back we come to a time before there were any written records at all. Until a nation has acquired an efficient alphabet, it must depend upon oral transmission; and it is obvious that if what, for want of another word, we must call "literature," depends for its continuing existence on human memories, the outlook for prose is bleak indeed. There may indeed be some rare souls (and I use the word "rare" in the sense of extremely infrequent) who are capable, like Macaulay or the winner of a $64,000 quiz, of humiliating feats of memory. But for most normal people it is much easier to recall an extended passage of verse than a corresponding piece of prose; and so, in an age when the transmission of literature depended upon the memory of scops and minstrels, it is not surprising that the great bulk of it should have been in verse. I am speaking, of course, of the kind of verse then being composed, which was marked by repetition and refrain, by the use of much conventional phrase and imagery, and by the openings it offered for improvisation. I should not find it at all easy to memorize Donne's *Second Anniversarie* or Dylan Thomas's *A Winter's Tale*; for in these poets the element of the conventional and the expected is almost non-existent, and their poetry has reached a degree of complexity, either of thought or of structure, which we do not find in the *Odyssey* or in *Beowulf*.

If we now consider our problem from the point of view of the writer rather than the reader, we shall find that when we go back to a time before written records existed the scales are again weighted in favour of verse rather than prose. The composition of poetry does not depend to any large extent on the poet's being able to write down his words on paper. Even in modern times it is the practice of many poets to compose their poems in the head, and to leave the transcription of the words until later: the paper stage is the stage of correction and of focussing the words and images. Wordsworth habitually composed his poems in the open air, and came into the house later to make a copy; and Boswell tells us that Johnson composed seventy lines of *The Vanity of Human Wishes* in one day "without putting one of them upon paper till they were finished."[2] It would be very surprising indeed to find that much prose was ever composed in this way; normally it is written by a writer hovering over a blank page with a pen or a pencil in his hand, and it is hard to see how it could be composed, except in the briefest passages, in any other way.

But we shall come closer to our problem if we now turn from the dawn of literature (about which, after all, anything we may say is bound to be more or less speculative), and move forward into historical times. Even in the middle ages, surprising as this may seem, the European writer in the vernacular seems to have found verse easier to write than prose. The poet was sustained and encouraged, as the prose writer was not, by working within a recognized form; he wrote in metre, and possibly in stanzas, which helped to shape and control his ideas and his expression of them. Compared with the poet, the prose writer was a pioneer venturing over fluctuating frontiers into the unknown, cutting his own path and blazing his own trail. He seems in consequence, when it came to framing his sentences, to have suffered from a sort of literary agoraphobia. In reading the English prose writers of the fourteenth and fifteenth, and even the sixteenth, centuries, we rarely feel that we are being taken straight to the point. As we follow our author, we find him constantly stumbling over obstacles, labouring along under every sort of difficulty, and frequently out of breath. In any passage of well-written prose there are always the shorter rhythm of the individual sentences and the longer rhythm of the general argument, and the two are mutually dependent. If the individual sentences have no tension, if they lie spread out before us like a collapsed tent, the writer's general argument will fail to emerge; and if his argument is not constantly present in his mind as he writes, the separate sentences will wander into every sort of digression and parenthesis and amplification. I quote a few sentences from William Roper's *Life of Sir Thomas More*, written about the middle of the sixteenth century:

Nowe while Sir Thomas Moore was Chauncellour of the Duchy, the sea of Roome chaunced to be void, which was cause of much trouble. For Cardinall Wolsey, a man very ambitious, and desirous (as good hope and likelyhood he had) to aspire unto that dignity, perceaving himself of his expectacion disapointed, by meanes of the Emperour Chareles so highely comendinge one Cardinall Adrian, sometyme his scholemaster, to the Cardinalls of Roome, in the tyme of their election, for his vertue and worthines, that thereuppon was he chosen Pope; who from Spayne, where he was then resident, cominge on foote to Roome, before his entry into the Citye, did put of his hosen and showes, barefoote and barlegged passing throwe the streates towards his pallaice, with such humblenes that all the people had him in greate reverence; Cardinall Wolsey, I say, waxed so wood therwith that he studied to invent all waies of revengment of his grief gainst the Emperour; which, as it was the begininge of a lamentable tragedye, so some parte of it as not impertinent to my present purpose, I recknid requisite here to put in remembraunce.

This Cardinall therefore, not ignorant of the kings inconstante and mutable disposicion, soone inclined to withdrawe his devotion from his owne most noble, vertuous, and lawfull wif, Queen Katherine, awnt to themperour, uppon every light occasion, and uppon other, to her in nobility, wisdome, vertue, favour and bewtye farre incomparable, to fixx his affection, meaning to make this his so light disposition an instrument to bring aboute his ungodly intent, devised to allure the kinge (then alredye, contrary to his mind, nothing les lookinge for, fallinge in love with the Ladye Anne Bullen) to cast fantasy to one of the Frenche kings Sisters: which thing, because of the enmity and warre that was at that tyme betweene the French king and the Emperour (whom, for the cause afore remembred, he mortally maligned) he was very desirouse to procure; and for the better atcheving thereof, requested Langland, Bishoppe of Lincolne, and ghostly father to the kinge, to put a scruple into his grace's head, that itt was not lawfull for him to marry his brother's wife: which the kinge, not sory to heare of, opened it first to Sir Thomas Moore, whose councell he required therein, shewing hym certaine places of scripture that somewhat seemed to serve his appetite; which, when he had perused, and theruppon, as one that had never professed the studye of divinity, himself excused to be unmeete many waies to medle with suche matters, the king, not satisfied with this awneswer, so sore still pressed upon him therefore, that in conclusion he condiscended to his graces motion.[3]

In this passage Roper has nothing particularly intractable to deal with; it is not the pressure of the thought that has become intolerable, but his inability to shape and order his material. I do not offer Roper as a writer fully representative of the sixteenth century; indeed, compared with his own father-in-law, whose life he is writing, he is something of a primitive. But his slow, laboured prose, with its parentheses, its subordinate clauses and phrases, its uncertain distribution of emphasis, and its desperate "Cardinall Wolsey, I say" inserted to pull the syntax together after it has become hopelessly involved, is characteristic of the loose and haphazard structure of English prose in the days when the prose writer, taking his pen in hand, rode forth on his adventurous quest like some gentle knight "pricking on the plaine."

The poet, on the other hand—and especially the poet writing in stanzas, as most of our poets in the fifteenth and sixteenth centuries were doing much of the time—had the great advantage of moving within prescribed limits. Working late in the fourteenth century with the seven-line stanza of *Troilus and Criseyde*, Chaucer was constantly encouraged to give his thoughts a shapely turn, and not to attempt more than the space at his disposal would permit. The same is true, if not so immediately obvious, in the poems he wrote in rhyming pentameters. But perhaps of all English poets Spenser shows most clearly how the stanza form continually influences a poet's thinking, and gently compels him to arrange his ideas in a lucid sequence. The nine-line stanza of *The Faerie Queene* allowed the poet considerable variety of expression; it could resolve itself into a number of different patterns. Unless Spenser lost control of the stanza or tried to force the thought into it (a circumstance which happens rarely indeed with this poet), that thought normally adapted itself to one or other of those rhythmical patterns, and sense and sound and rhythm coalesced indistinguishably. For an example we may take a passage in which Spenser is handling rather more thought than is usual with him. Artegall is replying to the Giant with the Scales, who has just been putting the case for what we should now call communism:

> Of things unseene how canst thou deeme aright,
> Then answered the righteous Artegall,
> Sith thou misdeem'st so much of things in sight?
> What though the sea with waves continuall
> Doe eate the earth, it is no more at all:
> Ne is the earth the lesse, or loseth ought,
> For whatsoever from one place doth fall,
> Is with the tide unto an other brought:
> For there is nothing lost, that may be found, if sought.

> Likewise the earth is not augmented more,
> By all that dying into it doe fade.
> For of the earth they formed were of yore.
> How ever gay their blossome or their blade
> Doe flourish now, they into dust shall vade.
> What wrong then is it, if that when they die,
> They turne to that, whereof they first were made?
> All in the powre of their great Maker lie:
> All creatures must obey the voice of the most hie.

> They live, they die, like as he doth ordaine,
> Ne ever any asketh reason why.
> The hils doe not the lowly dales disdaine;
> The dales doe not the lofty hills envy.
> He maketh Kings to sit in soverainty;
> He maketh subjects to their powre obay;
> He pulleth downe, he setteth up on hy;
> He gives to this, from that he take away.
> For all we have is his: what he list doe, he may.

> What ever thing is done, by him is donne,
> Ne any may his mighty will withstand;
> Ne any may his soveraine power shonne,
> Ne loose that he hath bound with stedfast band.
> In vaine therefore doest thou now take in hand,
> To call to count, or weigh his workes anew,
> Whose counsels depth thou canst not understand,

Sith of things subject to thy daily vew
Thou doest not know the causes, nor their courses dew.

For take thy ballaunce, if thou be so wise,
And weigh the winde, that under heaven doth blow;
Or weigh the light, that in the East doth rise;
Or weigh the thought, that from mans mind doth flow.
But if the weight of these thou canst not show,
Weigh but one word which from thy lips doth fall.
For how canst thou those greater secrets know,
That doest not know the least thing of them all?
Ill can he rule the great, that cannot reach the small.[4]

The thought here cannot be called complex; but how smoothly and clearly it is drawn out and expounded. The thought-rhythm of each stanza is different; but the adjustment of thought to rhythm and rhythm to thought is impeccable. Spenser had come to know the possibilities of his stanza so well that he could hardly go wrong, and as the ideas arose in his mind they accommodated themselves to that now familiar pressure. It may seem an odd thing to say of "the poet's poet," but the virtues of Spenser—the unfailing lucidity, the steady progress, the mind continually looking forward and organizing the argument—are the characteristic virtues of good prose.

To return to William Roper, it would be fair to say that his prose, like that of most of his English predecessors and many of his contemporaries, shows obvious signs of a lack of practice. The words come with difficulty because the whole process of composition is unfamiliar: Roper was doing something that he didn't often do. But why is it that men who can converse easily and naturally often find it so difficult to write? What stops them from writing as they speak? One possible answer is that if we wrote as we speak most of us would be writing poor prose, since in speaking we tend to convey much of our meaning by extra-literary means, and to pay comparatively little attention to the grammatical structure of our sentences. But again the difficulty may be due to a misconception of the nature of prose; to a notion that it is something altogether different from conversation, much more elaborate and artificial, more pondered and deliberate and formally balanced. It is quite true that prose is sometimes written in a highly conscious way, but it need not be; and it is not likely to be good prose unless the deliberation is natural to the writer, or has at least become second nature. For the writer of prose to assume, like M. Jourdain, that it has little or nothing in common with conversation is to invite failure. There is, however, a genuine difference between prose and conversation, and it does turn on the question of deliberation. The difference is one of *tempo*, and it accounts for the otherwise surprising fact that the good conversationalist is often a lame writer of prose. The writer who thinks too fast for his pen is apt to scatter his thoughts disconnectedly on the paper; although the ideas that enter his mind too rapidly to be written down may easily be skimmed off in conversation. On the other hand, the ideas might never occur to him at all without the stimulus of society to activate his brain. Conversely, the writer who thinks too slowly is likely not only to be a poor conversationalist, but in his writing to lose that momentum that keeps an argument (and the reader with it) moving steadily forward. In praising their fellow Shakespeare, Heminge and Condell remarked, on the evidence of his manuscripts, that "his mind and hand went together; and what he thought, he uttered with that easinesse, that wee have scarse received from him a blot in his papers."[5] Whether this is as true of Shakespeare as they thought, it certainly suggests the ideal *tempo* for prose writing. What the prose writer needs is a temperament nicely balanced between the sprightly and the phlegmatic, a lively mind and a deliberate judgment. His ideas will flow easily, but not too impetuously:

> Though deep, yet clear; though gentle, yet not dull;
> Strong without rage, without o'erflowing full.

Quite apart from the question of temperament, it is obvious that behind all effortless writing lies constant practice—in reading as well as in composition; and it is just this practice that Roper and most of his contemporaries must have lacked. The first book to be printed in England had appeared only about twenty years before Roper was born, and in the middle of the sixteenth century a collection of thirty or forty books probably represented a fair-sized private library. In such circumstances reading can hardly have become a habit: the books, more especially those in the vernacular, were not yet there in sufficient quantities to be read, and the habit of writing something every day had not yet become widespread.

In any case, the men of the fifteenth and early sixteenth centuries were writing before the rhythms of English prose had become firmly established. They had to make their own rhythms *all the time*. I do not wish to suggest that good prose is ever likely to be written by an author whose rhythm is not personal to him, and does not keep time with his thought; but it must obviously be easier for a writer to find his own personal rhythm when the basic rhythms of prose are already so familiar that they constantly come out to meet him when he is toiling with an idea to be expressed. In an age like the present, too, in which prose has become so common a form of expression, each new writer inherits a tradition of prose style, a way of turning his thoughts, and even—let us face it—a large number of useful *clichés* and idiomatic phrases, which will not—or, at least, should not—save him the trouble of thinking, but which will contribute largely to the facility of his writing. The roads are all there for the traffic to move along them: in Roper's day almost everything was still to do.

I have made so much of Roper's deficiencies that I ought to say one word more in extenuation of them: the merely physical frustration of writing on rough parchment with a quill pen may account for some of the difficulty that so many of our early prose writers seem to have experienced in expressing their thoughts. If such a suggestion seems fanciful, or even flippant, it should be remembered that the writer of prose is a good deal more dependent than the poet on physical conditions that allow the least possible interruption between the conception of the thought and the writing it down on paper. What, for example, would be the effect on the novelist's style if he were compelled, for want of other writing material, to write his novel on a schoolboy's slate—or, presumably, on a whole succession of slates? At all events, the manufacture of smooth paper, and the invention (in the seventeenth century) of pencils and steel pens, are not entirely negligible factors in the development of prose, however little the matter is capable of precise statement. There remains the possibility that what we call prose may have been dictated to an amanuensis, as Margery Kempe in the early fifteenth century dictated the story of her life to a clerk, or Henry James in the twentieth century his later novels to a secretary. Dictation constitutes a special circumstance which must considerably affect the mode of composition, but it has perhaps never yet been widely enough practised to have had more than a minor influence on English prose. What may happen with the increasing use of tape-recorders in the present century opens up an interesting field of speculation, but one which I shall not at present explore.

In making Roper representative of our earlier English prose, I may be doing it some injustice. I found what I wanted in Roper, those loose, sprawling sentences that wander like a river through marshy country, although it would not be difficult to produce many other examples from the writing of his contemporaries. Roper, it is true, may simply have been a rather muddled man whose sentences went to pieces because he failed to keep control of them. On the other hand, he may have been one of those writers who are almost unconscious of a reader, and still less of a listener, and whose prose is not, therefore, kept alert and lively by a desire to please, or (to put it at the lowest level) by an unwillingness to bore. If this is the truth about Roper, he was not necessarily characteristic of his period. Most of what is best in medieval literature—and this is as true of the poetry as of the prose—was written not to be read, but to be heard. "Of the few who could read," a modern scholar reminds us, "few [in the middle ages] were habitual readers; in any case, the ordinary man of our times probably sees more printed and written matter in a week than the medieval scholar saw in a year. . . . Further, as readers were few and hearers numerous, literature in its early days was produced very largely for public recitation."[6] Even in the sixteenth century, it has been suggested, a great part of the prose written was of "a public and oratorical" kind,[7] not addressed to the solitary reader, but intended for the ears of a listening assembly. Indeed, the prose in which the writer and the reader strike up a sort of private acquaintance is a comparatively late development, although of course some examples of it may be found quite early, usually in private correspondence, but occasionally elsewhere, as in the prefaces written for his various books by William Caxton. As soon as a writer begins to talk about himself he tends to become conscious of his reader: the "I" who is talking almost inevitably begets a "you" who is listening.

When a man is addressing an audience, or even when he is writing something like a course of lectures that is to be read to an audience, he adapts his discourse to the occasion. He can count, for one thing, on some part of his meaning being conveyed by certain modifications of the voice, by changes of intonation and emphasis, and also, if he is not a dreadfully inhibited person (in which case he probably ought not to be addressing an audience at all), by a certain amount of gesture and facial expression. With such aids to meaning, he can allow himself a fairly free construction, a more or less colloquial syntax. Whether a speaker sends an audience to sleep or holds its attention may depend upon the extent to which he has been able to modify the idiom of prose to suit the circumstances of public address. National tradition seems to play some part here. In general the American academic lecturer is apt to strike an English audience as being too formal; he reads to them what is in fact the typescript of an article ready for the press. Conversely, the English lecturer may seem too casual and offhand to the American audience. On the other hand, the American talking without premeditation into a microphone often seems to speak more naturally and idiomatically than the Englishman, who is apt to talk as if he were reading from a prepared script.*

---

*Perhaps he is. The effect, at all events, is often singularly inept. For example: "Well, here is Charlie Brown to say something about the League games.—What do you think of the prospects for this afternoon, Charlie?"— "Well, I expect the match between *Manchester United* and *Tottenham*

The most natural way of speaking, when our feelings are not deeply aroused, or when we are not trying to make an emotional impression of some kind, is to come out with the main idea at once, and then if necessary qualify it or modify it, and pass on to related ideas. Before the end of the fourteenth century, John Wyclif in his sermons had evolved a simple and unlaboured style of this kind for the exposition of the scriptures, and he carried the same directness and determination to be understood into his controversial writings.

If thou be a laborer, lyve in mekenesse, and trewly and wyllfully do thi labur; that if thi lord or thi mayster be an hethen man, that by thi mekenesse and wilful and trewe servise, he have not to gruche agens the, ne sclandre thi God ne Cristendom. And serve not to Cristen lordis with gruchying, ne onli in here presens, but trewli and wilfulli in here absens, not only for worldly drede ne worldly reward, but for drede of God and good conscience, and for rewarde in hevene. For that God that puttith the in such service wot what state is best for the, and wile reward the more than alle ertheli lordis may, if thou dost it trewli and wilfulli for his ordinaunce. And in alle thingis bewar of grucchyng agens God and his visitacion, in gret labour and long, and gret sikenesse, and other adversities, and bewar of wrathe, of cursyng and waryng, or banning, of man or of best. And ever kepe pacience and mekenesse and charite, bothe to God and man.[8]

What moulded Wyclif's prose was above all his consciousness of the humble listener, not there to be impressed, but to be helped and convinced. Preaching and talking frequently to such men and women, Wyclif was never tempted to put words before matter; indeed, he was under constant pressure to ensure that his words expressed the matter clearly and simply. But there was something else that his experience as a preacher must have taught him. The art of public speaking has no doubt altered

---

Hotspur to solve the relegation problem, and all the indications point to the *United* maintaining their unbeaten away record. Although *Blackpool* will be without the services of Matthews, I think they should have little difficulty in disposing of *Huddersfield Town*, having regard to the very capable forwards they have at their disposal and the superiority of their half-backs. At Stamford Bridge we should certainly witness a keen contest between *Chelsea* and *Luton Town. . . .*"

greatly from one age to another; we have only to read the sermons that appealed to past generations to realize how variously men have been moved by the spoken word. But there is at least one constant element in all good speaking: the successful preacher or orator must have a sense of timing. When he has this sense he does two things: he makes his discourse immediately intelligible, and, if he should wish to move as well as instruct his listeners, he gains a control over them that he could not otherwise obtain. It was just this sense of timing that we found to be so painfully absent from the prose of Roper; and it is perhaps a safe generalization to say that when we come upon prose written earlier than the seventeenth century that is still alive and capable of engrossing our attention, we nearly always find that it was written for an audience, or with an audience in mind, or, less commonly, with an actual or potential reader in view. The rhythms of the speaker may vary from the easily colloquial to something much more deliberate and artificial; but unless he can project his ideas in a rhythmical sequence, so that the rhythm of his sentences harmonizes with and reinforces the thought, he will leave only a faint or muddled impression on the minds of his listeners.

If it is self-evident that the sermons of Wyclif, and those of Latimer a century and a half later, were written to be heard, it is not perhaps so immediately obvious that other works, such as the *Travels* of the fourteenth-century Sir John Mandeville, were also intended for public recitation rather than solitary reading. In reading Mandeville we constantly meet with such phrases as "Now shall I tell you," "Now understandeth," "And ye shall understand," "But if it like you, I shall show," and so on, all of which suggest that the author was thinking in terms of a narrator reading aloud to a circle of listeners. Can we say the same of Malory's *Morte d'Arthur*, in which, about the middle of the fifteenth century, this simple medieval prose reaches perhaps its point of highest development?

And so as sir Mordred was at Dovir with hys oste, so cam kyng Arthur wyth a great navy of shyppis and galyes and carykes, and there was sir Mordred redy awayting uppon hys londynge, to lette hys owne fadir to londe uppon the londe that he was kynge over.

Than there was launchyng of greate botis and smale, and full of noble men of armys; and there was muche slaughtir of jantyll knyghtes, and many a full bolde barown was layde full lowe, on both partyes.

But kynge Arthur was so currageous that there myght no maner of knyght lette hym to lande, and hys knyghtes fyersely folowed hym. And so they londed magré sir Mordredis hede and all hys powere, and put sir Mordred abak, that he fledde and all hys people.

So whan thys batayle was done, kynge Arthure let serche hys people that were hurte and dede. And than was noble sir Gawayne founde in a greate boote, liynge more than halff dede. Whan kyng Arthur knew that he was layde so low he wente unto hym and so fownde hym. And there the kynge made greate sorow oute of mesure, and toke sir Gawayne in hys armys, and thryse he there sowned. And than whan he was waked, kyng Arthur seyde,

"Alas! sir Gawayne, my syster son, here now thou lyghest, the man in the worlde that I loved moste. And now ys my joy gone! For now, my nevew, sir Gawayne, I woll discover me unto you, that in youre person and in sir Launcelot I moste had my joy and myne affyaunce. And now have I loste my joy of you bothe, wherefore all myne erthely joy ys gone fro me!"[9]

I think we must suppose that Malory was writing for the individual reader, even though he knew nothing about William Caxton and that printing press of his which was soon to make it easier for readers all over England to hold a copy of the *Morte d'Arthur* in their hands. Yet his easy narrative style is based on the spoken language of the fifteenth century; and although Malory's rhythms are more gentle and more even and continuous than those of speech, we have the impression as we read that we are listening to a living voice.

In spite of the real differences which exist between conversation and prose writing, we need not for practical purposes make too absolute a distinction between the prose which is meant to be spoken and that which is composed by a writer who is addressing himself to a real or an imaginary reader. As readers, we can still be conscious of something that we may call the "voice" of the writer, even though that voice is to a large extent muted. Readers probably vary a good deal in the extent to which they are conscious, when they are reading silently, of the sounds of words and the rhythm of phrases and clauses and sentences; but if the effects are more rarefied some sensuous response is almost certainly present, and most readers are probably quick to distinguish between the writer whose prose at least recalls the living voice and the writer who has moved so far from idiomatic speech that his sentences never even suggest it. There is a kind of prose that might have come out of a machine; it may be clear, and it may convey meaning, but it has a bleak and impersonal quality that results from its having been composed in a kind of vacuum, with no particular reader in mind. This kind of prose may be found at any period; it is perhaps most often written by scientists. I offer an example from the nineteenth century.

If the persons forming a body-politic were mostly fixed in their positions, as are the units forming an individual body, the feeding of them would have to be similarly effected. Their respective shares of nutriment, not simply brought to their neighbourhood, would have to be taken home to them. A process such as that by which certain kinds of food are daily carried round to houses by a class of locomotive units, would be the universal process. But as the members of the body-politic, though having stationary habitations and working places, are themselves locomotive, it results that the process of distribution is effected partly in this way and partly by their own agency. Further, there results from the same general cause, a difference between the ways in which motion is given to the circulating currents in the two cases. Physical cohesion of the parts in an individual living body makes possible the propulsion of the nutritive liquid by a contractile organ; but lacking this physical cohesion, and lacking too the required metamorphosis of units, the body-politic cannot have its currents of commodities thus moved: though remotely produced by other forces, their motion has to be proximately produced by forces within the currents themselves.[10]

What Herbert Spencer appears to be saying in this passage is that the individual members of a community buy some of their food in shops, and have some of it delivered to their homes. The elaborate comparison with the physiological processes that go on inside the human body is not really necessary for making this quite simple point, but the author has committed himself to developing the analogy at length, and has already been labouring it for over fifty pages. Yet what gives the passage its anaesthetic effect is his almost inhuman use of language. Spencer's words have the glazed efficiency and something of the repellent property of bathroom tiles. He must, I suppose, be given the credit of wishing to make himself understood, but there his responsibility to the reader, and even his awareness of him, appears to end. He has no desire to please, to establish any human relationship with his reader; for to do so would be to disturb the scientific impersonality and generality of a world in which the milk-boy and the baker's boy are "locomotive units," delivering to other and more happily placed units in the body-politic, not the morning milk and rolls, but "their respective shares of nutriment."

At all periods in the history of English prose there have been individual authors who were able to speak easily and naturally to the reader, just as a successful speaker on the radio is able to establish a personal contact with the listener. But if this contact has always been possible, we shall find that it has apparently been more difficult to achieve in some generations than in others. The history of English prose is no doubt mainly a history of great prose writers, but it is also a history of fashions in writing. There are certain periods in our literature when the gap between writer and reader has been narrowed so much as to permit prose to approach the style of well-bred conversation, and other periods when the gap has widened so far as to leave the reader almost out of earshot. I do not wish at this stage to consider more closely the relationship between the prose and the spoken language of any historical period; but I am prepared to say dogmatically that such a relationship must always exist, and that prose which moves too far from the conversational idiom is always in danger of becoming laboured and artificial, and ultimately unreadable. The greater the psychological distance between writer and reader, the more likelihood there is that the writer will express himself stiffly and unidiomatically. It is true that the writer's awareness of the reader may lead to abuses—self-consciousness, self-display, facetiousness, tedious discursiveness, and so on; but to the writer who is not a spoilt artistic child the unseen presence of the reader acts as a valuable discipline, placing him under an obligation to express himself with lucidity and with reasonable brevity, and to think, like a good host, of his reader's pleasure and convenience rather than of his own.

II

So far we have been considering the problem of prose in more or less general terms. But in the earlier centuries of our literature there were certain special circumstances that made things more difficult for the writer of English prose. In the first place, it was not until about the end of the fourteenth century that English was established as the written language of the English people. After the Norman Conquest, Latin became for some time the official language, but in due course it was replaced by Norman French, the language spoken at court, in Parliament, and in the courts of law. Though the great mass of the English people still spoke their own tongue, French was the language spoken by their conquerors, and to a large extent the written language too. English, therefore, was mainly the language of the unlettered vulgar; it had little or no prestige, and it was rarely written. Worse still, it was broken up into such different dialects that communication between men living in different parts of the country presented some difficulty. The final triumph of the English language about the time of Chaucer synchronized with the general acceptance of the East Midland dialect as standard English, but even Chaucer, who wrote in it, is apprehensive that he may not be generally understood:

> And for ther is so gret diversite
> In Englissh and in writyng of oure tonge,
> So prey I God that non myswrite the,
> Ne the mysmetre for defaute of tongue.

> And red wherso thow be, or elles songe,
> That thow be understonde, God I beseche![11]

By 1400, however, the fight for the English language had been won; and the more English came to be written, the more the language became stabilized, for when a language is written down or recorded in print, it hardens into something permanent and standard much more quickly than when it is only spoken.

But here a second difficulty confronted English writers, and the prose writers more than the poets. If English had won the battle against Norman French, it had still, for literary purposes, to come to terms with an even more formidable rival—Latin. The prestige of Latin is not hard to understand; even today it still retains something of its old pre-eminence. But during the middle ages and the Renaissance, Latin was the language of learned men all over Europe; it was, as Dr. Johnson put it, "the parole of the learned," the language in which you wrote if you wished to be understood by educated men outside the frontiers of your own country. It was, too, the only language that had a vocabulary adequate for the discussion of theological, philosophical, scientific, and other learned subjects. The inadequacy of the vernacular was not a specifically English problem; it affected all the modern European nations to a greater or less extent, and in one country after another we can watch the linguistic resources being deliberately built up to meet the need for a fuller and more precise vocabulary. If a man had anything important to say, he tended to write in Latin, and only if he was consciously addressing himself to "meaner capacities" would he fall back on his mother tongue.* If you want someone to be a success at his job, you must give him responsibility; he will never get on if you trust him only in routine matters, and hand over all the important work to someone who is senior to him and more ex-

---

*There are some exceptions, of whom the most important in the fifteenth century are perhaps Reginald Pecock (1390?–1461?) and Sir John Fortescue (1394?–1476). Pecock's periods are often highly elaborate, and if some of his sentences have to be read twice before we can be sure of his meaning, the fault is not so much in their construction as in their formidable length. It is significant, too, that he is frequently driven to coin words to express his philosophical ideas.

perienced. Similarly, a language will never become fit for all occasions if it is used only for simple, everyday matters, and for the instruction or amusement of simple folk. Writing of medieval prose, W. P. Ker drew attention to certain limitations in it:

Prose literature taught and preached so much that it lost all spring and freshness; it suffered from an absorbing interest in the weaker brethren, and became too condescendingly simple. The childlike simplicity of medieval prose is sometimes a little hypocritical and fawning. Prose had been too long accustomed to talk down to its audiences.[12]

I have already praised the prose of Malory; but if the *Morte d'Arthur* is not quite a dead end, its prose is the culmination of a simple narrative style, and gives little promise of being able to deal with more abstruse matters. The main difficulty, however, was not so much one of sentence construction (though that comes into it) as of vocabulary. For several centuries Englishmen found themselves in the situation described by an early Elizabethan author of having "moe things than there are words to expresse things by."[13] If knowledge had remained stationary, the language would no doubt have caught up with the ideas to be expressed; but the Renaissance was a period of intense activity, when, as Richard Mulcaster put it, "the desire of learning enflamed studie, the longing for gain brought in great traffik, the delight to range did cause men travell, new occasions brought furth new words, as either more cunning made waie to more terms, or as strange devises did seke strange deliveries."[14] The English language had to be educated; it had to learn how to deal with new ideas.

Meanwhile, as late as the sixteenth century, the English author seems often to have wavered doubtfully between Latin and English. In the address to the Gentlemen and Yeomen of England in his *Toxophilus*, published in 1545, Roger Ascham expects that some people will blame him for having written his book in English. It would actually have been easier, he says, to write the book in Latin, and better for his reputation if he had done so; but by writing in English he has made himself intelligible to those whom he particularly wishes to read his book, the gentlemen and yeomen of England. And in any event, Ascham observes, if he writes in English he can hardly sink lower than those who have preceded him, since in the English tongue everything is written "in a maner so meanly, bothe for the matter and handelynge, that no man can do worse."[15]

There was clearly a vicious circle in the sixteenth-century linguistic situation. If English was ever to become a fully adult language, capable of conveying all that could be expressed in Latin, it would have to be used more and more frequently by the best minds; and yet the best minds tended to despise the vernacular and to write in Latin. The situation was made still more difficult by a constant outcry against "strange inkhorn terms"—the very words, as often as not, which were most badly needed, and which would have to be increasingly imported or invented, if English were ever to cope successfully with anything more than what Mulcaster called "home occasions." Naturally enough, if men wrote in English only when they wished (like Ascham on this occasion) to address the humbler and less educated reader, those inkhorn terms, since they would inevitably be unintelligible to the uneducated, would be an undesirable innovation; and yet, where no English equivalent existed, what was an author to do? It was all very well for Sir John Cheke to advise Sir Thomas Hoby that "our own tongue should be written clean and pure, unmixed and unmangled with borrowing of other tongues," since (as he argued) "if we take not heed by time, ever borrowing and never paying, she shall be fain to keep her house as bankrupt."[16] No doubt the borrowings had become so extensive by the middle of the sixteenth century that English was in some danger of losing its identity, but in the long run they were amply justified. We should never cease to be grateful that Shakespeare was born late enough to benefit from those linguistic innovations that Cheke deplored. If he had come into the world a generation earlier, Romeo and Hamlet, Ulysses and Prospero would all have spoken a homelier and less varied language. In his great speech on "degree" in Troilus and Cressida Ulysses would have been hard put to it to express his

meaning with the vocabulary available in the fifteenth, or even
the early sixteenth, century.

> But when the Planets
> In evill mixture to disorder wander,
> What Plagues, and what portents, what mutiny!
> What raging of the Sea! shaking of Earth!
> Commotion in the Windes! Frights, changes, horrors,
> Divert, and cracke, rend and deracinate
> The unity, and married calme of States
> Quite from their fixure! O, when Degree is shak'd,
> (Which is the Ladder to all high designes)
> The enterprize is sicke. How could Communities,
> Degrees in Schooles, and Brother-hoods in Cities,
> Peacefull Commerce from dividable shores,
> The primogenitive, and due of Byrth,
> Prerogative of Age, Crownes, Scepters, Lawrels,
> (But by Degree) stand in Authentique place?
> Take but Degree away, untune that string,
> And hearke what Discord followes: each thing meetes
> In meere oppugnancie. The bounded Waters,
> Should lift their bosomes higher then the Shores,
> And make a soppe of all this solid Globe:
> Strength should be Lord of imbecility,
> And the rude Sonne should strike his Father dead. . . .[17]

This passage is rich in abstract nouns; and though some of them
(e.g., *unity, degree, discord*) are of ancient origin, most of them
are coinages or importations dating from the sixteenth century.
Words which, according to the *Oxford English Dictionary*, date
from the fifteenth century are: *mixture, commotion, enterprize.*
But many more came into the language at the very period when
the protest against inkhorn terms was at its loudest: *disorder*
(1530); *portents* (1563); *mutiny* (1567); *designes* (1588, in
Love's Labour's Lost); *commerce* (1537); *imbecility* (1533).
Three of the words in this passage date from the early years of
the seventeenth century: *fixture, primogenitive,* and *oppugnan-
cie*; the two last, which are not recorded earlier than *Troilus and
Cressida*, are probably of Shakespeare's own coinage. Of words
other than nouns there are: *divert* (1548); *deracinate* (1599 in

Henry V); and *dividable* (1587). Without this rich new vocabulary the English language would have been in the condition in which Hobbes visualized the life of man: "poor, nasty, brutish, and short."

Nor is it merely that Shakespeare would have had a smaller and more monosyllabic vocabulary at his disposal: but he would inevitably have been inhibited by the defeatist attitude to the English language that was so prevalent in the days of his father and grandfather. "Consciousness of the unliterary nature of the medium of expression," as we have recently been reminded, "induced in those who wrote in English a kind of inferiority complex."[18] By the time Shakespeare was reaching manhood, this distrust of English had largely given way to a new sense of its limitless possibilities. "Bliss was it in that dawn to be alive," but to be young with Marlowe, Nashe and Shakespeare was "very heaven."

The linguistic situation in the middle ages and the early Renaissance amounted to a sort of bilingualism. There is always the sort of bilingualism, as we have already seen, which comes from assuming a complete gap between prose composition and conversation, and so prevents a man from writing as he would speak. But in the fourteenth century there was also the bilingualism that results from a man habitually speaking in French or in his own dialect and trying to write what was gradually becoming standard English; and in the fifteenth and sixteenth centuries there was the kind of bilingualism that comes from a man doing most of his writing, and, as a schoolboy, much of his talking, in Latin.* Lest I may seem to exaggerate about the Latin, it should be remembered that the grammar-school boy not only spent most of his school hours learning Latin, but was also taught in Latin, and made to speak Latin to his fellow pupils in school hours. If the little victim lapsed into his native English, retribution was swift. "It is a usual custom," wrote John Brinsley, whose *Ludus Literarius* was published in 1612, "to appoint

---

*The situation in the middle ages was a good deal less desperate than this. In the thirteenth and fourteenth centuries the teaching in English schools appears to have been either in French or in English.

custodes or *asini*, . . . to observe and catch those who speake English in each fourme, or whom they see idle, to give them the *ferula*, and to make them *custodes* if they cannot answer a question which they aske."[19] This system of schoolboy informers may not be pretty to contemplate, but it was probably highly efficient. Since no one wanted to be a *custos*, and since the only way to escape was by catching someone else out (as in the old game of Spy Fox), you naturally kept your ears open for anyone who cheated and spoke English. At this formative stage, when the boys might have been learning to express themselves fluently in their own tongue, the insistence that they should converse habitually in Latin (and what Latin it must often have been!) can only have inhibited them when they came to speak and write in English. Brinsley was well aware of this danger. When children first take up Latin, he remarks, "many of them will forget to reade English, and some of them bee worse two or three yeares after they have been in construction, than when they began it." He would like to give them instruction in English reading, but "this I cannot possibly doe, but they must needs bee hindred in their Latine."[20] Latin is indeed a language so different in construction from English that the sort of facility expected of the sixteenth-century schoolboy was almost enough to produce a split linguistic personality. The predicament might have been much worse if the Latin had been better; but there is in fact a good deal of evidence to show that the English schoolboy often wrote Latin with a word order resembling that of his native language.

At all events, the almost exclusive concentration on Latin persisted right through the seventeenth century, and was still dominant in the eighteenth century. One of the few scholars to raise any sort of protest was John Locke: "And since 'tis English that an English Gentleman will have constant use of, that is the Language he should chiefly cultivate, and wherein most Care should be taken to polish and perfect his Style." But that, Locke continues, is just what does not happen: "If any one among us have a Facility or Purity more than ordinary in his Mother Tongue, it is owing to Chance, or his Genius, or any thing

rather than to his Education, or any Care of his Teacher."[21] For
several centuries, then, English boys were taught to express
themselves in Latin, seldom if ever in English. Unless we are
to be cynical, and doubt the possibility of ever teaching boys to
write at all, we must conjecture that the want of any instruction
in English composition could only have had an adverse effect on
the national literature. It is perhaps unlikely that there were
many mute, inglorious Hookers or Jeremy Taylors or Swifts,
men who would have done great things if only they had received
instruction in the writing of English prose; the great writer, we
must suppose, will always make himself heard, provided he has
had some sort of education in literature. But English prose might
certainly have developed faster, and the general level of writing
might have been a good deal higher, if for several centuries
English boys had not been left to find out more or less for themselves how to frame an English sentence, and how to develop a
consecutive argument in their own language.

It is true, however, that in every age there have been simple
and unsuspecting people who have failed to realize that prose is
somthing that can be written only by the erudite, and who have
therefore expressed themselves without self-consciousness and
with an idiomatic directness that seizes upon and holds the
attention. Historians of literature have often noted that behind
all the fashions of prose there remains an unpretentious style
which is used by humble men who have something that they
want to say. "Men who owed little or nothing to French or
Latin," we have recently been told by a writer on fifteenth-
century prose, "were constantly attempting to put down their
thoughts in a clear and unornamented fashion. They have little
to offer the seeker of 'fine' prose; their only endeavour was to
state their ideas in a straightforward fashion, almost as simply
as if they were talking."[22] In the Elizabethan period, we are
assured by another writer, "we find that many an author,
whether because he followed the principle of decorum or because
he was unlearned in the terms of rhetoric, wrote the plain prose
of instruction in such subjects as arithmetic, cookery, horse-

breeding, or plain narrative in many a first-hand account of discovery and travel by sea and land. Those who are content merely to state matters of fact, especially important matters of fact, are almost immune from rhetorical fashions. The prose of the Anglo-Saxon chronicle can be matched through the centuries."[23] In prose, as in other things, it is often the meek who inherit the earth; they write well because, as Johnson put it, they "speak only to be understood." In the passage from which those words come Johnson is advancing a theory to account for the existence of a mode of speech that never goes out of date; and what he has to say applies equally well to prose composition:

If there be, what I believe there is, in every nation, a stile which never becomes obsolete, a certain mode of phraseology so consonant and congenial to the analogy and principles of its respective language as to remain settled and unaltered; this style is probably to be sought in the common intercourse of life, among those who speak only to be understood, without ambition of elegance. The polite are always catching modish innovations, and the learned depart from established forms of speech, in hope of finding or making better; those who wish for distinction forsake the vulgar, when the vulgar is right; but there is a conversation above grossness and below refinement, where propriety resides. . . . [24]

Many of the most famous names in English prose belong to Johnson's category of the "polite" (Lyly, Sidney, Halifax, Chesterfield, Peacock, Thackeray, Henry James), or his category of the "learned" (Hooker, Andrews, Donne, Sir Thomas Browne, Johnson, Gibbon), and the prose of at least some of those authors has become a curiosity, or a splendid monument to a vanished or vanishing past. But there are other writers equally famous—Bunyan, Defoe, Cobbett, Hazlitt, spring at once to the mind—whose prose has its origin in "the common intercourse of life," and, because it was never fashionable or learned, has never gone out of fashion. I will not draw the moral that the prose which comes nearest to idiomatic conversation is always and necessarily the best, for that would be to narrow the range of English prose drastically, and to apply a utilitarian test to writers who had other ends in view. But the prose of men who write "almost as simply as if they were talking" has a power of surviving as living discourse which is often denied to the authors of more artificial and studied prose. They, too, survive in their own fashion, but it is as literary landmarks, to be visited occasionally and walked round and examined with curiosity, but not to be read (as we normally read our own contemporaries) with an immediate and continuous absorption of what is being said, and with an almost complete unconsciousness of their style as style.

Style, of course, is not just a patina that gathers on the surface of old prose; but when we become too conscious of style it is either because the writer himself was too conscious of it while he was writing, or because his prose is already moribund and is beginning to give off the characteristic aroma of antiquity. "The words in prose," Coleridge once remarked, in contrasting prose and poetry, "ought to express the intended meaning, and no more; if they attract attention to themselves, it is, in general, a fault. In the very best styles, as Southey's, you read page after page, understanding the author perfectly, without once taking notice of the medium of communication—it is as if he had been speaking to you all the while."[25] For some people this is a hard saying, and they will wish to reject what they feel to be a puritanical attempt to limit too strictly the frontiers of prose. But are they not, perhaps, objecting to what prose, at its most characteristic, is and does? It is significant that almost all the words derived from the term "prose"—prosaic, prosy, prosiness, prosify, and so on—have a derogatory meaning that suggests an unwillingness to accept prose for its own sake: prose is *not* poetry. Prose, however, exists in its own right, and, as we shall see later, it is a different form of discourse from poetry, carrying the reader forward in a continuous movement, and with an immediate and developing awareness of the writer's ideas. Good prose is that which conveys those ideas to the mind of the reader most fully and precisely, and with the least impediment or interruption. Prose, it may be said, should be heard and not seen; when the reader begins to see too clearly what made it work, it is no longer working.

III

In what follows I shall be chiefly concerned with tracing the
main stream of English prose through the centuries. To some it
may seem impossible to discuss prose usefully in this way at all.
The word itself covers almost everything written that is not
verse, and prose style is therefore an abstract conception of
almost limitless variety. I have constantly to remind myself that
any critical consideration of prose style must take into account
not merely the words on the printed page, but the occasion for
which they were written, the reader or readers to whom they
were addressed, and the intention of the writer. Two of the most
intelligent critics of English prose, Sir Herbert Read in *English
Prose Style* and Professor Bonamy Dobrée in *Modern Prose
Style*, have approached their subject with such considerations
constantly in mind; and it may well seem that to discuss English
prose without reference to the occasion and the intention is, at
the best, unprofitable, and at the worst, misleading. Certainly
the criticism of any specific passage of prose is not likely to
penetrate very far unless such considerations are present in the
mind of the critic. We must be prepared to find Lord Bacon
writing in one style in his *Essays*, in a different style in *The
Advancement of Learning*, and in still another fashion in *The
New Atlantis*. Again, there is often a world of difference between the way an author writes in public and in private. Who,
for example, is the author of the following letter?

DEAR BETTY,

Though it were no wonder this very tempestuous and stormy
winter, yet I am sorry you had such an uncomfortable sight as to
behold a ship cast away so near you. This is no strange, though
unwelcome, sight at Yarmouth, Cromer, Winterton, and sea towns.
Though you could not save them, I hope they were the better for
your prayers, both those that perished and those that 'scaped. Some
wear away in calms, some are carried away in storms; we come into
the world one way, there are many gates to go out of it. God give us
grace to fit and prepare ourselves for that necessity, and to be ready

to leave all when and howsoever He shall call. The prayers of health are most like to be acceptable; sickness may choke our devotions, and we are accepted rather by our life than our death; we have a rule how to lead the one, the other is uncertain and may come in a moment. . . .[26]

The father who is writing to his daughter in that letter is Sir Thomas Browne, and though his theme is death, the style has little resemblance to that of *Urn Burial*: the occasion, the reader, and the author's intention are all different. But when we have made every allowance of that kind, it still remains true that prose is subject to certain pressures at different periods and runs after certain fashions, and that the way a man writes will depend to a considerable extent on the century in which he was living and writing, the social class into which he was born, the sort of education he received, and even at some periods on the religion he professed. It is with such considerations in mind that we can best follow the progress of English prose from the sixteenth century to the present day.

II. APES AND PEACOCKS

THE PROSE WRITERS of the middle ages and the early Renaissance had still much to learn; but, at their best, they had mastered instruction and description, and they were in full command of their resources in a straightforward narrative of action. When they had a story to tell in a simple time sequence they wrote easily, and sometimes, as in the *Morte d'Arthur*, with a leisurely and unemphatic rhythm which establishes a sense of continuity, and has something of the hypnotic effect, without the regularity, of metre. On the other hand, when they had no story to tell, no events to narrate—and sometimes when they had— they were apt to flounder and to lose themselves in a maze of subordinate clauses and parentheses; their sentences grew by a process of agglomeration rather than organically. When they were left to make their own thought-sequences, they were apt to become involved in difficulties of syntax, and at times to break down completely. Although, as I have suggested, the natural method of speaking or writing is to come out with your main idea first, and then to amplify or qualify it as secondary ideas arise in the mind, such a method has its limitations. As soon as the thought becomes complex, and passes beyond simple relationships to involved conceptions, there is a likelihood that natural and spontaneous expression will become inadequate, and that some degree of artifice will be forced upon the writer.

So far as English literature is concerned, the movement towards a more conscious and artificial prose style becomes fully noticeable about the middle of the sixteenth century, and it is part of a general literary development that affected all the nations of Europe. The movement originated in a renewed study of the classical writers, more especially of Cicero, and in the ambition of Renaissance scholars to write as fine Latin as those ancient authors whom they admired so profoundly. It is well known that Lord Bacon viewed this humanistic enthusiasm for Latin composition with a rather disapproving eye, and listed it, indeed, among the diseases of learning. "Men began to hunt more after words than matter," he complains in *The Advancement of Learning,*

more after the choiceness of the phrase, and the round and clean composition of the sentence, and the sweet falling of the clauses, and the varying and illustration of their works with tropes and figures, than after the weight of matter, worth of subject, soundness of argument, life of invention or depth of judgment.

He cites as examples "the flowing and watery vein" of Osorius, and the learned imitations of the German Ciceronian Sturm; and he comes nearer home:

Then did Car of Cambridge and Ascham with their lectures and writings almost deify Cicero and Demosthenes, and allure all young men that were studious, unto that delicate and polished kind of learning. . . . In sum, the whole inclination and bent of those times was rather towards copie than weight.[1]

Those Cambridge scholars, then, were infecting the younger generation with a passion, not for English prose, but for the prose of Cicero; and when they wrote in Latin, they tried to be as Ciceronian as they could, both in their vocabulary and in the structure of their sentences.

What it meant to be Ciceronian is not easy to state in a few words; but in general it meant using the most "classical" Latin, cultivating the periodic and balanced sentence, and satisfying the ear with a cadence that was not, it is true, completely regular, but none the less easily recognizable and agreeably harmonious. The Ciceronian period is necessarily the result of deliberation; it demands a careful placing of words and phrases, in the interest both of meaning and of euphony, but, in an inflected language, of euphony more than meaning. It is not difficult to understand how the cleverer schoolboys and university students, and so in

their turn mature scholars, might take to the writing of Ciceronian prose as an intellectual game, and devote far less attention
to what they were saying than to the way they said it. Indeed,
the moment you begin consciously to imitate the style of any
other writer, the expression is likely to take precedence over the
matter to be expressed. You have put the cart before the horse;
or rather, you have become so much interested in horsemanship
that you have gone capering off on the horse's back, and left the
cart stranded on the road. In a famous dialogue, *Ciceronianus*
(1528), Erasmus makes the Ciceronian describe his procedure:

. . . I consult all the lists; I select some words strikingly Ciceronian,
some tropes, and phrases, and rhythms. Finally, when furnished
sufficiently with this kind of material, I examine what figures of
speech I can use and where I can use them. Then I return to the
question of sentences. For it is now a work of art to find meanings
for these verbal embellishments.[2]

The Ciceronian, Erasmus implies, has got all the stylistic bits
and pieces; he then looks about for an excuse to use them, and
the only importance of any meaning that he can think up is that
it gives him the chance to display his skill as an imitator of
Cicero's style. Stylistically, it might be said, he has got the
Oxford accent. The *Ciceronianus* is satire, no doubt; but for
those of us who can recall with what smug satisfaction we used
to work a *quippe qui* or a *haud multum abfuit quin* into our
Latin proses at school, not really very far from the truth.

But what has all this imitation of Cicero got to do with the
writing of English? Modern English is not to any large extent
an inflected language, and the word order necessarily differs
widely from that of Latin. An author who tried in English to
imitate too closely the periods of Cicero would end by producing
something that was unidiomatic and that read like a poor translation. To some extent this is what actually happened with sixteenth-century prose writers who had received the usual classical
education of those days. On the other hand, it is only fair to say
that any boy who has been taught Latin intelligently should
emerge from this discipline with a quickened sense of the natural

word order of his own language; for it is part of his task not only
to be able to read Latin, but to render it into idiomatic English.
Medieval and early Renaissance pupils were encouraged to find
the best English equivalent for the Latin by the various *vulgaria*
used in the schools.[3] These were similar to the modern English-
French or English-Italian phrase books which are available at
railway terminals for the English traveller setting off on a Con-
tinental holiday. We need not therefore assume that when the
classically educated student turned from writing Latin to writing
English he had everything to learn and to unlearn. He had, in
fact, acquired much that he could turn to good account. Even
though his own language was very different from Latin, he had
learnt from Cicero and other classical writers how to build a
balanced sentence, how to distribute the emphasis, and how to
express his thought so that the cadence of the phrases and clauses
helped to make the idea easily intelligible.

At all events, English prose in the sixteenth century is marked
by a conscious effort to write in English with the same care as
the scholar gave to writing in Latin. Historians of English literature have duly noted this new elaboration of our prose; but in
seeking to account for it they have forgotten one obvious fact.
If you are conscious, as Ascham and many other sixteenth-century scholars were, that your national prose is lame and impotent,
no doubt the first step to making it better will be to provide the
writer with an adequate vocabulary; and that, as we have seen,
was being done all through the sixteenth century, and even
earlier. But the second step is equally important. If you wish to
raise the general level of prose composition, you cannot do better
than base your style on the artificial, periodic prose of the
Ciceronians, for that sort of writing is the easiest to learn and
to teach. It can be taught because it is to a large extent a matter
of rule and methods; it offers a number of moulds for expressing
ideas, and those can be applied (though not without some loss
of what is individual and immediate) to any particular idea.
What cannot be taught, and takes much longer to acquire, is the
style that follows every turn and twist of the writer's mind; for
in such writing the form is whatever gives unimpeded expression

to the idea, and the rhythm is, as nearly as that is ever possible, the rhythm of the thought. If such a style is to avoid mere impressionism and disconnected jotting, the writer has to be really thinking, and not just day-dreaming or doodling with ideas. But this style will also make a greater demand than the periodic style upon the intelligence and alertness of the reader, for it leaves him with much more to do for himself. In modern literature it is often the style of the writer who is not especially concerned with readers, but who is bent on getting something expressed exactly as he experienced it, and who may therefore take little trouble to make things easy for his readers, either by preparing them for what is to follow, or by indicating the transitions of his thought. It is certainly unlikely to be a successful style in a period when prose is still feeling its way uncertainly towards a conventional and settled construction.

The balanced and periodic type of sentence, then, a sentence marked frequently by inversion and suspension of meaning, was the sixteenth century's answer to the often ill-constructed and even shapeless prose that had preceded it. In its earlier manifestations it has sometimes the sort of crudity that the innovator finds it so difficult to avoid. A naïve and significant example of the new artificiality, eagerly attempted but only half-learnt, occurs in the opening sentence of Edward Hall's *The Union of the Two Noble and Illustre Famelies of Lancastre and Yorke* (1542):

What mischiefe hath insurged in realmes by intestine devision, what depopulacion hath ensued in countries by civill dissension, what detestable murder hath been committed in citees by seperate faccions, and what calamitee hath ensued in famous regions by domestical discord and unnaturall controversy: Rome hath felt, Italy can testifie, Fraunce can bere witnes, Beame can tell, Scotland maie write, Denmarke can shewe, and especially this noble realme of Englande can apparently declare and make demonstracion.

This is the prose of a writer who is determined to be elegant and shapely at all costs; it has the exaggerated effect that we usually meet with in a new fashion, and that is later modified into something less obvious and emphatic when the fashion has established itself. Hall's elegant variation (breaking down only once when he unaccountably repeats the word "ensued") has all the marks of a writer who, as Ascham observed of Sallust, has "an uncontented care to write better than he could."[4] What Ascham has to say about Hall shows that by 1570 his prose already seemed crude to a younger generation:

Nevertheles, some kinde of *Epitome* may be used, by men of skilful judgement, to the great proffet also of others. As if a wise man would take *Halles* Cronicle, where moch good matter is quite marde with Indenture Englishe, and first change strange and inkhorne tearmes into proper and commonlie used wordes: next, specially to wede out that, that is superfluous and idle, not onelie where wordes be vainlie heaped one upon an other, but also where many sentences, of one meaning, be so clowted up together as though *M. Hall* had bene, not writing the storie of England, but varying a sentence in Hitching schole. . . .[5]

Compared with the prose of Hall, that of John Lyly is sophisticated; yet Lyly has something of the monotonous excitement of a child blowing on his new tin trumpet. Before we criticize the men of the sixteenth century too severely, however, we should remember how much, one way or another, they did for English prose. If in their first enthusiasm they shaped it too artificially, they must be given full credit for having broken away from the old rambling and inconsequential sentences that overflowed in all directions. All writing, it may be said, rests upon some kind of adjustment between the thought and the means at the writer's disposal for expressing it: the Ciceronians only differed from other writers in the extent to which the thought was made to accommodate itself to a shapely form, and at this point in the development of English prose their too consciously balanced periods were an invaluable discipline.

If sixteenth-century prose owes much to the conscious imitation of Latin authors, it owes perhaps still more to the rhetorical training that the English schoolboy received; a training that gave him a far livelier awareness of the figures of speech, and indeed of the whole art of writing, than the average boy or girl is likely to get today. This instruction in the art of rhetoric gave the Elizabethan writers most of their stylistic devices, and, equally important, it provided them with a body of readers able to understand and appreciate what they were doing. Yet the Elizabethans undoubtedly carried their love of rhetoric too far, and in the hothouse atmosphere of the later sixteenth century the growth is at once too exuberant and too exotic. In reading Elizabethan prose we are frequently apt to feel that the energy expended is in excess of the occasion; the thing would have been said better if it had been said more simply. In the prose of John Lyly so much care has been given to tropes and turns that inevitably we pay comparatively little attention to what has been said—not, I hasten to add, that we probably lose much by our inattention. Rather than quote from *Euphues*, I choose a passage from one of his plays:

As much difference as there is betweene Beautie and Vertue, bodies and shadowes, colours and life; so great oddes is there between love and friendshippe. Love is a Camelion, which draweth nothing into the mouth but ayre, and nourisheth nothing in the bodie but lunges: beleeve mee, Eumenides, Desire dyes in the same moment that Beautie sickens, and Beautie fadeth in the same instant that it flourisheth. When adversities flowe, then love ebbes; but friendshipp standeth stifflie in stormes. Time draweth wrinckles in a fayre face, but addeth fresh colours to a fast friende, which neither heate, nor cold, nor miserie, nor place, nor destiny, can alter or diminish. O friendship! of all things the most rare, and therefore most rare because most excellent, whose comforts in misery is alwaies sweet, and whose counsels in prosperitie are ever fortunate.[6]

James Mill, the father of John Stuart Mill, is said to have remarked after reading the philosopher Kant: "Oh ay, I can see what poor Kant would be at." After reading such a passage as that from Lyly, we probably feel that we know what poor Lyly would be at. The passage has most of the characteristics of his prose: balance and antithesis carried to a point where they become monotonous, and reinforced by corresponding sound effects ("fair face . . . fast friend") and by a rhythmical correspondence in the phrases and clauses. With all this goes a certain amount of conscious repetition (for Lyly can never be accused of rushing his fences), and an air of leisurely deliberation which is directed more to the words than to the matter. The words seem often to be more important to Lyly for their sound than for what they say: we may feel, for example, that adversities only "flow" because love "ebbs," and that there is little reason to suppose that friendship is ever menaced by heat or cold—unless we take those words in a metaphorical sense, in which case there is surely every reason to believe that anger or indifference might diminish, or even kill, friendship.

Lyly's effects, it may be objected, are altogether too obvious; he is a primitive, with all the exaggeration of primitives. Perhaps we shall do better if we turn to Sir Philip Sidney.

So that the third day after, in the time that the morning did strow roses and violets in the heavenly floore against the coming of the sun, the nightingales (striving one with the other which coulde in most dainty variety recount their wrong-caused sorow) made them put off their sleep, and rising from under a tree (which that night had bin their pavilian) they went on their jorney, which by and by welcomed Musidorus eyes (wearied with the wasted soile of Laconia) with delightfull prospects. There were hilles which garnished their proud heights with stately trees: humble valleis, whose base estate seemed comforted with refreshing of silver rivers: medows enameld with all sorts of ey-pleasing floures: thickets, which being lined with most pleasant shade, were witnessed so to by the cherefull disposition of many wel-tuned birds: each pasture stored with sheep feeding with sober security, while the prety lambs with bleating oratory craved the dams comfort: here a shepheards boy piping, as though he should never be old; there a young shepherdesse knitting, and withall singing, and it seemed that her voice comforted her hands to work, and her hands kept time to her voices musick.[7]

That is a far more subtle and delicate prose than Lyly's. If there is still a rather formal balance, especially in the second sentence, it is much less obtrusive and triumphantly regular than is usual with Lyly. Sidney is more likely to be blamed for a tendency to over-decorate, to cover the plain statement with a fanciful filigree (as when the morning strews "roses and violets in the heavenly floore"), to overwork his epithets, and more especially such

double adjectives as "eye-pleasing" and "well-tuned." The Elizabethans had an almost childlike delight in the flowers of rhetoric. They never took to heart the old maxim of *ars est celare
artem*; indeed, they felt a naïve pleasure in parading their artistic
skill. Ben Jonson's remark about Shakespeare, "His wit was in
his own power; would the rule of it had been so too," would
often be a fair enough comment on the prose of Sidney, and
still more on that of Nashe. Both of those writers "flowed with
that facility, that sometimes it was necessary it should be
stopped."[8]

The *Arcadia*, written as Sidney explains in the dedication to
his sister, "in loose sheetes of paper, most of it in your presence,"
may remind us again that a writer, at his most elaborate and
artificial, can still be addressing himself to an actual reader. Even
the balanced Ciceronian period, however far it may depart from
the conversational, is a form of discourse; it speaks to us in the
voice of the formal orator, and has its own special power of
stirring the emotions and holding the attention. What sort of
effect it may have is made clear by Longinus when he is dealing
with "hyperbaton," which he defines as "a disturbance of the
proper sequence of phrases or thoughts." He singles out Demosthenes for special praise:

For he often leaves suspended the thought with which he began,
and interposes, as though he struck into a train of reasoning foreign
to it and dissimilar, matter which he rolls upon other matter, all
drawn from some source outside, till he strikes his hearer with fear that
an entire collapse of the sentence will follow, and forces him by mere
vehemence to share the risk with the speaker: then, when you least
expect, after a long interval, he makes good the thought which has
so long been owing, and works in his own way to a happy conclusion: making the whole a great deal more impressive by the very
hazard and imminence of failure which goes with his Hyperbata.[9]

Since the ancient world was so much concerned with the art of
persuasion, it is not surprising that the effect of the orator on
his hearers, or of the writer on his readers, should have been so
frequent a point of departure for classical criticism.

If Bacon was in no doubt at all about the tendency of Ciceronianism to make men think too much about the words and too
little about the matter, his attitude to the rhetorical structure
of Ciceronian prose is not quite so simple. He is aware that "the
round and clean composition of the sentence, and the sweet
falling of the clauses" may become ends in themselves; but he
knows, too, that for the ready conveyance of ideas into men's
minds, and for obtaining belief, some recourse to elocution is
almost inescapable. It would be strange indeed if the author of
The Advancement of Learning had thought otherwise; for he
was himself a noble orator, whose hearers "could not cough or
look aside from him without loss," and who "had his judges
angry and pleased at his devotion."[10] When, therefore, we find
Bacon apparently denigrating eloquence, and giving his approval
to a very different kind of expression, we must remember that
almost everything that he said on such matters is to be found
in *The Advancement of Learning*, where he is concerned with
the possibility of increasing the sum of human knowledge by
means of scientific discovery, and with the accurate statement of
scientific observations. In seeking to make science "come home
to men's business and bosoms," Bacon naturally made use in
his own *magnum opus* of all the eloquence at his command; but
if any man had a scientific discovery to record, Bacon expected
him to "transplant it into another, as it grew in his own mind."[11]
On the other hand, by using "methods" (by which Bacon meant
"the regular, systematic arrangement of literary materials"), "a
man shall make a great shew of an art, which, if it were dis-
jointed, would come to little"; and to make it quite clear what
he has in mind, he quotes from *Ars Poetica*, 242–3: "such is the
power of order and connexion, such the beauty that may crown
the commonplace." "Methods," he continues, "are more fit to
win consent or belief; but less fit to point to action; for they
carry a kind of demonstration in orb or circle, one part illuminating another, and therefore satisfy; but particulars, being dispersed, do best agree with dispersed directions."[12] What Bacon is
saying here is that the rounded period, the artificial and balanced
sentence, carries conviction with the reader and wins his assent

simply because it *is* rounded and balanced, because it all hangs together and comes to an expected conclusion. It is accepted because it sounds right. This style of writing, as he observes in an earlier passage, is "magistral and peremptory, and not ingenuous and faithful; in a sort as may be soonest believed, and not easiliest examined."[13]

Is it, then, undesirable that the writer should try to assert his power over the reader? Or alternatively, does there come a point at which control passes into tryranny, and the reader ceases to think for himself, or is at least discouraged from doing so? It is true that the effect—and sometimes the intention—of the eloquent prose that Bacon has in mind is often much less to make the reader think, than to keep him from disagreeing. The writer of this kind of prose, as Dryden said of the author of a heroic play, endeavours to establish an absolute dominion over the mind of his reader.[14] He obtains that dominion partly by the inevitability of his rhythms, and partly by the sound of the words he uses and his careful placing of them in the sentence. The result may be that the reader will do what Wordsworth thought so many readers of poetry habitually do: he will expect to be borne along "like an Indian prince or general—stretched on his palanquin."[15] The simple-minded reader, at least, is only too easily impressed, particularly, of course, when to the certainty and grandiloquence of the rhythm is added the pomp of a polysyllabic vocabularly. The dangers of this sort of writing are beautifully demonstrated by Peacock in a lively passage in *Headlong Hall*:[16]

MR. ESCOT: I presume, sir, you are one of those who value an *authority* more than a reason.

MR. PANSCOPE: The authority, sir, of all these great men, whose works, as well as the whole of the *Encyclopaedia Britannica*, the entire series of the *Monthly Review*, the complete set of the *Variorum Classics*, and the *Memoirs of the Academy of Inscriptions*, I have read through from beginning to end, deposes, with irrefragable refutation, against your ratiocinative speculations, wherein you seem desirous, by the futile process of analytical dialectics, to subvert the pyramidal structure of synthetically deduced opinions, which have

withstood the secular revolutions of physiological disquisition, and
which I maintain to be transcendentally self-evident, categorically
certain, and syllogistically demonstrable.

SQUIRE HEADLONG: Bravo! Pass the bottle. The very best speech
that ever was made.

MR. ESCOT: It has only the slight disadvantage of being unintelligible.*

Squire Headlong has obviously some affinity with the old lady
who loved "that blessed word 'Mesopotamia'"; but there are
many who are prepared, like him, to yield to sound what they
cannot give to sense. Yet if the eloquent style can be abused
when it is used to conceal poverty of thought, it is also the
natural and almost inevitable style when the matter to be
delivered is weighty and complex. "But what!" as Sidney said,
"Shall the abuse of a thing make the right use odious?"[17]

A very different sort of style is required when, as Bacon put
it, we wish to "point to action" (by which I think he means
when we wish to make men think, and proceed to further
inquiry), and when we are concerned with recording particular
facts. "Knowledge that is delivered as a thread to be spun on,"
Bacon argues, "ought to be delivered and intimated, if it were
possible, in the same method wherein it was invented"[18]: that
is, it should describe, as closely (as "ingenuously and faith-
fully") as possible, the actual history of the discovery. Such a
style is not concerned to persuade, but to elucidate; it will
follow the windings of a man's thought, and the reader will be
conscious only of the matter expressed, never of the manner.

It must be added that Bacon wrote comparatively little of
that sort of prose himself; he preferred in the *Advancement* to
use all the resources of rhetoric to recommend it. His own most
characteristic writing has in it much of the "magistral and
peremptory": the reader sits back and allows him to take
control. When he is pleading the cause of learning in the
Advancement, he is the conscious advocate, and his argument
comes rolling forward in a succession of great waves. Learning,

*I can testify to the effectiveness of Mr. Panscope's speech. Many years
ago I memorized it, and used it in a school debate to depose with irrefragable
refutation against the arguments of my opponent.

he tells us, civilizes men's minds, it takes away all levity and rashness of judgment, it prevents thoughtless admiration, and it gives men a sense of proportion:

So certainly, if a man meditate much upon the universal frame of nature, the earth with men upon it (the divineness of souls except) will not seem much other than an ant-hill, whereas some ants carry corn, and some carry their young, and some go empty, and all to-and-fro a little heap of dust. It taketh away or mitigateth fear of death, or adverse fortune; which is one of the greatest impediments of virtue, and imperfections of manners. For if a man's mind be deeply seasoned with the consideration of the mortality and corrupt-ible nature of things, he will easily concur with Epictetus, who went forth one day and saw a woman weeping for her pitcher of earth that was broken; and went forth the next day and saw a woman weeping for her son that was dead, and thereupon said: *Heri vidi fragilem frangi, hodie vidi mortalem mori.*[19]

Here, surely, we have the sort of writing that carries "a kind of demonstration in orb or circle"; its strength is more than the sum of its parts, for one part is constantly "illuminating another." There is much of this noble oratory in Elizabethan prose, in the writing of Bacon himself, in Hooker, in Raleigh, in Donne. What especially characterizes it, in contrast with the prose of some later writers in this balanced and periodic style, is its happy combination of regularity with variety. In the pas-sage just quoted the reader has all the feeling of inevitability that this kind of prose invariably gives, but experiences little of the monotony that so often accompanies it. Bacon's rhythm arouses an over-all expectation, but carries within it many minor surprises; and in such passages as "whereas some ants carry corn, and some carry their young, and some go empty, and all to-and-fro a little heap of dust," it responds delicately to the thought and feeling, and awakens a parallel response in the mind of the reader.

II

I have already suggested that for thought which has arrived at some degree of complexity, recourse to the periodic structure is almost inevitable, since the relationship of one idea to another cannot be adequately shown if the writer tumbles down his thoughts just as they arise in his mind. Quite apart, therefore, from any literary fashion that led writers to imitate Cicero and to concentrate their attention on the structure of their sentences, the increasing complexity of the thought to be expressed by such writers as Bacon and Hooker, and by such preachers as Donne, would have led necessarily to a prose marked by a considerable degree of elaboration and artifice, if they were to make their meaning clear. Bacon may be right about the "magistral and peremptory" character of this sort of prose, but that is perhaps more often the effect than the intention. If we are to grasp the full significance of the movement in the sixteenth century towards a more elaborate and formal prose style, we must keep in mind the very nature of prose composition, and the way in which the words and phrases used by the writer build up his meaning in the mind of the reader. With such considerations in mind, it may be permissible to suggest that the new formal prose of the sixteenth century is related to a steady increase in the reading public, and so to a corresponding acceleration in the tempo of reading. The rapid reader, as I shall hope to show, is best served by a page of balanced and "artificial" prose, for the simple reason that he has to read less of it to grasp the meaning.

The medium of the speaker is articulated sounds in time; the medium of the prose writer is the printed page, in which visual symbols replace the spoken words, but recall, to varying degrees with different readers and in different literary contexts, the words when they are spoken aloud. If every word of a speaker, and still more every syllable, impinged as a separate unit of sound on our consciousness, we should have the greatest difficulty in following his discourse. Even if he spoke with exaggerated slowness, that very slowness—such is the force of custom—would make him almost unintelligible. But of course words are not normally heard in that way; they group themselves together into phrases and clauses, and from the rise and fall of the speaker's voice, his changes of pace and emphasis and so on, an audience is able to anticipate, within limits, what he is going to say next. The listener is like a tennis player on the other side of the net adapting his stance to the next stroke of his opponent. Similarly, a practised reader is hardly conscious of the individual words on the page, and still less of the letters that form each word; his eye passes rapidly across the print in an almost continuous absorption of the writer's meaning, gathering in whole clauses and even sentences much more quickly than they could ever be spoken; we even hear of some readers who can take in a whole page at a glance—or, at any rate, who say, and presumably believe, that they can. How, then, is this done? The rapid reader is obviously not reading *verbatim*: he catches the writer's meaning, not by paying close attention to every word in a sentence, but by attending to certain hints that the writer has given him. The writer will go on to complete his clause or sentence, but the rapid reader has already seen what is coming, and has passed on to the next sentence. In a sense, the better a man writes, the less you need to read him. If the reader is confronted with a shapeless sentence—by Caxton, or Roper, or anyone else—he cannot be sure that he has the meaning until he has read every word. If, on the other hand, a sentence has a good formal structure, if the words and phrases are strategically placed, and if one point leads easily to the next, the meaning can be grasped without difficulty.* When a man read, at most, a dozen books in the course of a year, he could afford to give his time to jogging along with a Caxton or a Fabyan; but when reading became a habit, and books were competing with one another for attention, the author had to be prepared to do more for his reader. The increasing tendency in modern prose to use short sentences is symptomatic of a general speeding up in the act of *reading*.

Still, the ability of the good prose writer to carry his reader along with him in a continuous and developing movement of thought is something so remarkable that it is only because we

*Cf. John Hoskins, writing about 1600: "For the consequence of the sentences, you must see that every clause doth, as it were, give the cue to the other and be, as it were, spoken before it come" (*Directions for Speech and Style*, ed. Hoyt H. Hudson [1936], p. 4).

have become accustomed to it that we take it for granted. The wonderfulness of prose struck Coleridge so forcibly one day that he was moved to jot down a note about it in the book he had just been reading.

Not having my pocket book, I take note here of what has just struck my feeling, namely, that . . . prose must have struck men with greater *admiration* than poetry. In the latter it was the language of passion and emotion; it is what they themselves spoke and heard in moments of exultation, indignation, etc. But to have an evolving roll, or a succession of leaves, talk continuously the language of deliberate reason, in a form of continued preconception, of a Z already possessed when A is being uttered,—this must have appeared *god*-like. I feel myself in that state when in perusal of a sober, yet elevated and harmonious, succession of sentences and periods, I abstract my mind from the particular passage, and sympathize with the wonder of the common people who say of an eloquent man, "He talks like a book."[20]

The kind of writing that particularly impressed Coleridge was that which we meet with continually in such authors as Hooker and Isaac Barrow. The following passage from Hooker has all the god-like control—that sense of "Let there be light, and there was light"—which Coleridge admired:

He that goeth about to persuade a multitude that they are not so well governed as they ought to be, shall never want attentive and favourable hearers; because they know the manifold defects whereunto every kind of regimen is subject, but the secret lets and difficulties, which in public proceedings are innumerable and inevitable, they have not ordinarily the judgement to consider. And because such as openly reprove supposed disorders of state are taken for principal friends to the common benefit of all, and for men that carry singular freedom of mind; under this fair and plausible colour whatsoever they utter passeth for good and current. That which wanteth in the weight of their speech is supplied by the aptness of men's minds to accept and believe it. Whereas on the other side, if we maintain things that are established, we have not only to strive with a number of heavy prejudices deeply rooted in the hearts of men, who think that herein we serve the time, and speak in favour of the present state, because thereby we either hold or seek preferment;

but also to bear such exceptions as minds so averted beforehand usually take against that which they are loth should be poured into them.[21]

Beside that passage from Hooker we may put one from Isaac Barrow's sermon, "Against foolish Talking and Jesting," written two generations later for a Restoration congregation. We must distinguish legitimate jesting, Barrow says, from that foolish talking to which St. Paul took exception:

And such a resolution seemeth indeed especially needful in this our age (this pleasant and jocular age), which is so infinitely addicted to this sort of speaking, that it scarce doth affect or prize any thing near so much; all reputation appearing now to vail and stoop to that of being a wit: to be learned, to be wise, to be good, are nothing in comparison thereto; even to be noble and rich are inferior things, and afford no such glory. Many at least, to purchase this glory, to be deemed admirable in the faculty, and enrolled among the wits, do not only make shipwreck of conscience, abandon virtue, and forfeit all pretences to wisdom, but neglect their estates and prostitute their honour: so to the private damage of many particular persons, and with no small prejudice to the public, are our times possessed and transported with this humour. To repress the excess and extravagance whereof, nothing in way of discourse can serve better than a plain declaration when, and how, such a practice is allowable or tolerable; when it is wicked and vain, unworthy of a man endued with reason, and pretending to honesty or honour. This I shall in some measure endeavour to perform.[22]

Such writing is possible only for an author who is capable of sustained thought, and who can hold in focus a complex of ideas. He must have what Coleridge called "that prospectiveness of mind, that surview, which enables a man to see the whole of what he is to convey appertaining to any one point; and by this means so to subordinate and arrange the different parts according to their relative importance, as to convey it at once as an organized whole."[23] Hooker's prose has a grave dignity that is characteristic of him; but it may be questioned whether Barrow's reach of mind and copiousness of expression are not even more remarkable. It must be added that as the range of both writers was much above the ordinary, their prose sometimes makes considerable demands upon the attention of the reader; but they can hardly be blamed for that. "Hooker's style," as Fuller remarked, "was long and pithy, driving on a whole flock of several clauses before he came to the close of a sentence. So that when the copiousness of his style met not with a proportionable capacity in his auditors, it was unjustly censured for perplexed, tedious, and obscure."[24] If Hooker's periods come rolling in like a succession of Atlantic waves, it is because his thought has the weight and volume that naturally gathers itself up into such cumulative aggregations of meaning.

III

It would be wrong to give the impression that the artificial and periodic style which established itself in the sixteenth century completely drove out the simpler and more colloquial prose of earlier days. In the novels of Deloney, in the last pamphlets of Robert Greene, in the Martin Marprelate tracts, in Harrison's *Description of Britayne*, in Arthur Dent's *The Plaine Mans Pathway to Heaven*, and in many other practical books and treatises, the writing is often direct and simple. So long as he is addressing himself to the common reader, the Elizabethan has the chance to write without ostentation, though even then he does not always take it. Too often Elizabethan prose—the prose of Nashe and much of Dekker, for example—seems to be designed to impress, or it is the prose of men who are poets and have no intention of forgetting it.

Nashe's prose raises the question of what the prose writer can fairly expect of his reader. No doubt the constant reading of newspapers in the twentieth century has led us to assume that we should be able to take in a page of print with the minimum of attention, and in that respect we may be worse readers than the Elizabethans, who read much less, and who must therefore have read more slowly, and presumably more carefully. But if a piece of prose is not necessarily meant to be read once only, it is normally expected to yield most of its meaning at a first reading. Poetry we approach with a rather different attitude. The first reading of a poem may leave us with only an imperfect realization of what it says or means; but because we have obtained some impression of its structure, and because it *is* poetry and our whole approach to poetry is conditioned by a different sort of expectation, we are prepared to read it a second and a third time, and even, if the experience seems likely to be worth it, to go on reading until our understanding is complete. We will do this for prose only to a limited extent. Most of us are willing to re-read a sentence if its full significance has escaped us; but we will not readily give it a third or fourth chance.

The trouble with Nashe is partly that he is a good deal less interested in making things easy for the reader than in enjoying his own superiority over him; or, if that seems too harsh a judgment, in exploiting the linguistic resources of the language for his own amusement. He takes more delight in self-expression than in communication. English literature is big enough to absorb one Nashe; but if all our writers insisted on showing the same wilful eccentricity, English prose would be a tropical jungle in which the unfortunate traveller would wander in hopeless confusion. Those brisk and lively young Elizabethans, bent all the time on being themselves, pouring forth their wit in abundance and revelling in imagery and conceit, were a brilliant and turbulent coterie of individualists, but their talents were more suited to poetry and poetic drama than to prose. After reading a few pages of Nashe one begins to have a new respect for dullness. This is Nashe re-telling in his own happy-go-lucky fashion the old story of Hero and Leander:

Hero hoped, and therefore she dreamed (as all hope is but a dream); her hope was where her heart was, and her heart winding and turning with the wind, that might wind her heart of gold to her, or else turn him from her. Hope and fear both combatted in her, and both these are wakeful, which made her at break of day (what an old crone is the day, that is so long a breaking) to unloop her luket or casement, to look whence the blasts came, or what gait or pace the sea kept; when forthwith her eyes bred her eye-sore, the first white whereon their transpiercing arrows stuck being the breathless corps of Leander: with the sudden contemplation of this piteous spectacle of her love, sodden to haddock's meat, her sorrow could not choose but be indefinite, if her delight in him were but indifferent; and there is no woman but delights in sorrow, or she would not use it so lightly for everything.

Down she ran in her loose night-gown, and her hair about her ears (even as Semiramis ran out with her lie-pot in her hand, and her black dangling tresses about her shoulders with her ivory comb ensnarled in them, when she heard that Babylon was taken) and thought to have kissed his dead corpse alive again, but as on his blue jellied sturgeon lips she was about to clap one of those warm plaisters, boistrous woolpacks of ridged tides came rolling in, and raught him from her (with a mind belike to carry him back to Abydos). At that she became a frantic Bacchanal outright, and made no more bones but sprang after him, and so resigned up her priesthood, and left work for Musaeus and Kit Marlowe.[25]

In this passage Nashe is making much play with words (*sudden . . . sodden; indefinite . . . indifferent*), and with ideas (the *transpiercing arrows* of Hero's eyes stick in the *white*, not of a target, but of Leander's lifeless body). The Elizabethan author is unusually liable to be distracted by the very words he is using; they are so new and so fresh to him that they seem to make a physical impact upon his consciousness, bringing with them all sorts of sensuous associations which are apt to lead him into every sort of decorative irrelevance. On any page of Nashe we are pretty sure to find some striking phrases: the drowned Leander *sodden to haddock's meat*; Semiramis, *her black dangling tresses about her shoulders with her ivory comb ensnarled in them*; the *boistrous woolpacks of ridged tides*, and so on. In poetry such phrases would be in their natural environment, for the poet expects a full sensuous response from his reader, a willingness to re-create from the words of the poem what it feels like to be a drowned man floating in the sea, or how the sea looks when the long waves are breaking in white foam on the beach. The poet can count on getting this sort of response from his reader because poetry is normally read much more slowly and attentively than prose, and with a total response to the connotations as well as to the denotations of words, to their sound and rhythm, and to the images singly and in relation to the other images. The poem (at any rate if it is a short lyric) is held in suspense in the reader's mind, and he receives a complex and simultaneous impression from all its parts.

I would not wish to suggest that the prose writer is not interested in imagery, in the connotations of words, and in their sound and rhythm; but he is working under different conditions, and he cannot count on the same sort of co-operation, or even attention, that the poet gets. The reader of prose expects to be carried forward in a fairly rapid and steady movement, and anything that seriously checks his progress will destroy that sense of continuity and progressive development upon which the effect of prose largely depends. Nashe, however, is constantly making insistent demands upon his readers for a complex response which inevitably retards their advance, and may even bring them to a standstill. A phrase so packed and pregnant with suggestion as *boistrous woolpacks of ridged tides* cannot be taken in at a glance; it must inevitably bring the reader to an admiring pause, until, consciously or subconsciously, he has worked out its implications. Nashe has managed to combine the turbulent movement of the sea (*boistrous tides*) with the straight, sculptured effect (*ridged*) of a wave visually arrested, so to speak, at some particular moment of its advance towards the shore. The whole clause, *boistrous woolpacks of ridged tides came rolling in,* owes a good deal of its effect to the way in which the vowels and consonants and the over-all rhythm suggest a wave thundering upon the beach, the two heavily stressed monosyllables (*ridged tides*) giving a sense of great waves pounding on the shore. The word *woolpack* was used by Elizabethan sailors to describe a large mass of foaming water; it suggests buoyancy and the fleecy white of a breaking wave, and so adds to the total visual and kinetic effect. From all those separate sensory impressions, of sound, movement, substance, shape, colour, together with such secondary impressions as may come from *boistrous* and *woolpacks,* the reader has to build up a total impression of considerable complexity and hold it focussed in his consciousness. And this is only one such passage of many. The *blue jellied sturgeon lips* of the drowned Leander make almost equal demands upon the reader's ability to respond to the sound and suggestion of the words. Nashe is a sort of Prodigal Son of English literature, and no one will grudge him his fatted calf; but the normal work of prose has to be carried on by writers of a less boisterous and more disciplined character.

IV

Although the Ciceronian style survived among some of the more learned writers, such as Milton, well into the seventeenth century, a reaction had already set in by the beginning of the century, and again it was a Latin writer who served as the model to be imitated. This writer was Seneca; although Tacitus, too, had his imitators. The conscious recommendation of the style of Seneca may be said to begin in the last quarter of the sixteenth century with the French scholar Muret, and with the Dutch scholar Lipsius, who edited both Seneca and Tacitus. When, in 1580, Montaigne brought out the first two books of his *Essais*, written in a manner that recalled some of the features of Seneca's prose, the Senecan style spread rapidly.

In trying to estimate the influence of Seneca we have to face the fact that his admirers were not in agreement as to what constituted his peculiar excellence. He was praised for two different reasons. To Lipsius, he was the great master of brevity: "His words are choice, suitable, and significant; they always mean something more than they actually say. And this seems a special genius of his, that in an economy of words he was a wonderful force and efficacy; in brevity he has clearness and brilliance." Although Lipsius is aware that Seneca's prose is by no means unpremeditated, he yet insists that "while you recognise artistic construction, you will admit no feminine artificiality, and it is for fighting and the arena that the whole equipment is made, not for pleasure and scenic show."[26] To Montaigne, on the other hand, what is most admirable in Seneca is not so much his terseness and succinctness, as the absence of a formal and artificial balance, and the suggestion in his apparently loose and desultory prose of a mind in the act of thinking. Montaigne was no admirer of oratory, and he seems to have had a particular distaste for Cicero. The kind of writing that pleased him best was intimate, confessional, revealing the mind and personality of the writer; private rather than public, tentative and exploratory rather than magisterial. The growing preference for the Senecan style in the late sixteenth and early seventeenth centuries is not just another example of the whirligig of taste; it reflects a new interest in human personality, the interest of the writer in himself and in those outside himself, and it occurs most significantly, perhaps, in such new seventeenth-century forms as the "character" and the essay. The anti-Ciceronians, Professor F. P. Wilson has said,

looked for a style that should be more in keeping with the spirit of free inquiry into the morals of men or the secrets of nature which they desired, a style that preferred intimate discourse to public oratory, one that could stop and brood, present the mind in process of meditation, turn upon itself to hint a doubt, indicate that knowledge was not yet a circle, a style that whether terse or loose would avoid copiousness and place matter before words.[27]

Seneca's English imitators reproduce either the brevity and point, or the looseness and informality. Bishop Hall, who earned the title of "our English Seneca," does both. His succinct, pointed style may be seen in the following character of the Covetous Man:

He is a servant to himselfe; yea to his servant; and doth base homage to that which should be the worst drudge. A liveless peece of earth is his master, yea his God, which he shrines in his coffer, and to which he sacrifices his heart. Every face of his coine is a new image, which he adores with the highest veneration; yet takes upon him to be Protector of that he worshippeth: which he feares to keepe and abhorres to lose; not daring to trust either any other god, or his owne. Like a true Chymist he turnes every thing into Silver, both what hee should eat, and what he should weare; and that he keeps to looke on, not to use. When he returnes from his field, he askes, not without much rage, what became of the loose crust in his cup-bord, and who hath rioted among his Leekes. . . .[28]

The old rolling periods have disappeared. Hall is jerking and stabbing at the reader's attention, giving him no rest, forcing him either to concentrate on what is being said, or else to throw the book down in despair. What the reader cannot do with such prose is to lie back and let the pealing organ go sounding through the nave and the aisles.

As with the Ciceronian style, so with the Senecan we find every degree of imitation, from those who ape Seneca to those whose writing is only lightly influenced by him. The pointed style is commonest among the character writers, such as Bishop Earle, and, later in the seventeenth century, Samuel Butler. The looser and more desultory style is well seen in Robert Burton, who tells his reader that he has

> writ with as small deliberation as I do ordinarily speak, without all affectation of big words, fustian phrases, jingling terms, tropes, strong lines, that like Acestes' arrows caught fire as they flew, strains of wit, brave heats, elogies, hyperbolical exornations, elegancies, etc. which many so much affect. I am . . . a loose, plain, rude writer, *ficum voco ficum, et ligonem ligonem*, and as free as loose, *idem calamo quod in mente*, I call a spade a spade, . . . I respect matter, not words, . . . I neglect phrases, and labour wholly to inform my reader's understanding, not to please his ear; 'tis not my study or intent to compose neatly, which an Orator requires, but to express myself readily and plainly as it happens.[29]

To show the sort of influence that Seneca could still exert comparatively late in the seventeenth century, I quote a passage from a little-known author, David Lloyd. He is writing in 1665 about the Earl of Essex:

> He was a masterpiece of Court and Camp; his beauty enamelling his valour, and his valour being a foil to his beauty, both drawing those noble respects of love and honour; both aweing, both endearing. It was his nobleness that he distrusted none, it was his weakness that he trusted all; whereby he suffered more from those that should have been his friends than from those who were his enemies. Good

man! his ruin was that he measured other breasts by his own; and that he thought mankind was as innocent as his own person. His merit gained applause, and his parasites swelled it to popularity; and the last enjealousied that Majesty which the first had obliged. His youthful and rash sallies abroad gave too much opportunity to his enemies' whispers, and too visible occasions for Her Majesty's suspicion, that he was either weak, and so not to be favoured; or dangerous, and so to be suppressed. Absence makes princes forget those they love, and mistrust those they fear. Exact correspondence is the sinew of private and public friendship. So great a master he thought himself of his sovereign's affection, that he must needs be master of himself and steal to France without leave, where, said the Queen, he might have been knocked on the head as Sidney was. . . .[30]

Lloyd was a young man when he wrote this, a clever young Oxford scholar with a turn for writing; but already he was, stylistically, rather behind the times. The new prose being written by Dryden and others in this period is much less mannered, and nearer to good conversation than the pointed and studied brevity of Lloyd's Senecan style.

By the second decade of the seventeenth century the Senecan influence had become sufficiently noticeable in England for Bacon to remark upon it in his *De Augmentis Scientiarum* (1623). In describing the new style Bacon observes:

Little better is that kind of style . . . which near about the same time succeeded this copy and superfluity of speech. The labour here is altogether that words may be aculeate, sentences concise, and the whole contexture of the speech and discourse rather rounding into it self than spread and dilated. So that it comes to pass by this artifice, that every passage seems more witty and weighty than indeed it is. Such a style as this we find more excessively in Seneca; more moderately in Tacitus and Plinius Secundus; and of late it hath been very pleasing unto the ears of our time.[31]

It will be seen that while Bacon disapproved of Ciceronianism, he was "little better" satisfied with Senecanism. He was a hard man to please; and again his criticism was at variance with his practice, for many of his own essays were written in a modified form of the Senecan style. Yet he was not inconsistent. Since it led to a kind of writing which seemed "more witty and weighty" than it actually was, the Senecan style only encouraged writers to hunt in a different fashion "more after words than matter." Ultimately, Bacon objected to both styles because they *were* styles and turned men's attention from things to words. What he wanted we have already seen: "knowledge . . . delivered and intimated, if it were possible, in the same method wherein it was invented."[32] This comes very close to the stylistic aims of the Royal Society as described by Bishop Sprat; a style in which "men delivered so many things almost in an equal number of words."[33] It is an impossible ideal (Bacon's "if it were possible" is significant); but it came nearer to being realized in English prose after 1660 than it had ever been before.

So far as the influence of Seneca is concerned, it was probably most effective and lasting where it led to a freer and more conversational mode of expression than where it encouraged pointedness and brevity; when, in fact, writers followed the example of Montaigne rather than that of Lipsius and his followers. It might be expected that we should be able to trace the influence of Seneca on the prose writers of the Restoration period and the early eighteenth century, and perhaps it is not altogether impossible to do so. But as we move further away in time from the sixteenth-century and early seventeenth-century imitators of Seneca, it becomes more and more difficult to isolate any influence that he may still have exerted. The prose of Dryden and Halifax, and later of Addison and Swift, is the prose of men who are not aping any other writer, ancient or modern; it is the product of new literary and social conditions, and it is to these that we must now turn.

III. THE AGE OF PROSE

THE GREAT PROSE WRITERS of the Elizabethan and Jacobean ages, and the Caroline writers after them, were mostly scholars, and their prose has more of the atmosphere of the study than of the world of men and affairs. To the natural remoteness, or, at any rate, aloofness,* of a writer like Sir Thomas Browne has been added the further distancing of three centuries, and what was always slightly odd and antiquarian has become quaint and antiquated. When we read his *Religio Medici* or *Urn Burial* we may well be delighted by the curious workmanship; but the books themselves belong to a past that now seems far away (a past that they share with Jacobean furniture), and in consequence we may be in some danger of paying more attention to their style than to their substance. The prose of Browne, like that of Jeremy Taylor, will always have a peculiar attraction for the connoisseur, to whom style is capable of becoming an end in itself, and of imparting, in the words of Walter Pater, "a special, a unique, impression of pleasure."[1]

Yet there are other prose writings of the same period which retain much more clearly the accents of a living voice; and if it is not the voice of the twentieth century, it still speaks to us in words and rhythms that we can associate with daily life and with our common human concerns. A new prose was emerging in the seventeenth century, simpler, less ornate, more colloquial, more practical, and pitched at such a level that it could make sense,

---

*Writing to Sir Kenelm Digby, 3 March, 1643, about *Religio Medici*, Browne stated that it was "contrived in my private study, as an exercise unto my self, rather than exercitation for any other" (*Works*, ed. Geoffrey Keynes [1928–31], VI.271).

and immediate sense, to the average man. It is customary to date this change from about 1660, but in fact the development begins earlier; it cannot be satisfactorily explained unless we take several contributing factors into account. To some extent the Senecan influence which we have already considered led to a new directness of expression, but not necessarily to simplification or immediate intelligibility. The new prose is rather the result of a conscious reaction from the language of scholars; and it reflects, too, the very circumstances which made the old scholarly mode of writing either impracticable or unattainable.

The first and most obvious fact to be remembered is that, as the seventeenth century proceeded, more and more men and women wanted, or needed, for one reason or another, to write. Since most of these new writers were not scholars, and since what they had to say was often of the utmost importance to them, they naturally tended to express themselves in a language not much removed from the one in which they spoke. Such prose, of course, had been written in similar circumstances before the seventeenth century; it is to be found, for example, in the narratives of English seamen collected and published by Richard Hakluyt in 1589, as it was to be found again at the close of the seventeenth century in the *Voyages* of William Dampier. If there is any new circumstance to be taken into account here, it is only that the number of such writers was steadily increasing with a general growth of the population and a gradual rise in the level of education.

But there were certain new developments in the seventeenth century which encouraged the growth of a vigorous and colloquial prose. One of the most important was the outburst of political and religious journalism (the two adjectives are often barely distinguishable at this period) during the Civil War and the years immediately preceding and following it. The journalist has to write fast; and although we cannot assume that when a man writes fast he will necessarily write simply, since leader-writers and civil servants apparently write fastest when they use a pompous and abstract jargon of their own, and it takes time to be simple, yet the seventeenth-century journalist is usually at his

THE AGE OF PROSE

simplest and most natural when he has least time to elaborate
and embroider his argument. What produces the jargon of the
modern leader-writer and civil servant is largely boredom: the
dreary necessity of grinding out yet another editorial or compil-
ing yet another report. But with seventeenth-century England
split from top to bottom into rival camps of Royalists and Puritans, the issues were tremendously alive, and men spoke and
wrote from burning conviction. The Puritans, it is true, developed in due course a biblical jargon of their own, but at least
it was not the circumlocutory and abstract journalese of the
nineteenth and twentieth centuries, echoing like hollow re-
verberations in an empty hall. The seventeenth century is in
general free from such faults because it was a century of belief
and violent controversy.

As an example of the brisk, workmanlike prose so frequently
written during the Civil War, we may look at a passage from the
first number of the royalist periodical, *Mercurius Aulicus*
(1643). The author, Sir John Berkenhead, has a lively tale to
tell, and he is in no danger of spoiling it in the telling, because
what he has to record was at least a mild success for the Royalists.
Sir John Byron had been sent with a troop of horse to Burford
to convey two cart-loads of ammunition to the Marquess of
Hertford, and he suddenly found himself with a skirmish on his
hands:

A musket or two went off, and thereupon the Alarme was given
that the Rebels were entred into the towne already. On this Sir John
taking the next horse that came to hand, armed with his sword onely
went towards the market place: where meeting his Lieutenant
Colonell, hee commanded him to take a competent number of horse,
and make good the bridge, lest if the enemy had tooke it the way
might have been stopped betwixt him and the Marquesse; the Ammunition being sent meane time, with a guard of 30 horse towards
Stow, where the Marquesse was that day expected, as before was
said. By this time it was known for certain both by the fire and by
the report of the Muskets that the Rebels were about the White
Hart, being an Inne in the utmost part of the Towne, from whence
a lane leadeth to the Market Crosse. And therefore making thither

with all the speed he could, he found the lane full of Musketeers, who were ready to enter the High Street, and the guard of horse which had been left there, retreating as well as they could out of the danger of the shot. Sir John considering hereupon, that should the enemy possesse the Crosse, and the houses on either side the streete, it was not possible for him to continue there, nor do any service with his horse against them being sheltered and defended, commanded those who were next to follow him, and rushed in upon them, laying about him with his sword, for other weapons hee had none, as was said before. No sooner was he got amongst them, but some of those which were furthest gave fire upon him; which doing no hurt, they presently betooke themselves to flight in a great confusion, some crying that they were for the King, and some for Prince Rupert. In this confusion he drave them before him to the further end of the lane where the Inne standeth, into which they ran: and into which he entring pell-mell with them, received a blow on the face with a Pole-axe or Holbard, wherewith he was in danger to have fallen from his horse. But quickly recovering himselfe againe, he saw the Inne-doore full of Musketeers, and himselfe alone unarmed and naked of defence in the open street, and thereupon returned backe to the market crosse, where he found his men, who had mistaken his command conceiving that they were to have tarried there to make good that place. Upon his comming backe, Captain Apsley rid up to the Inne-doore, which he entred with much danger but no hurt; a Trooper of Sir John's being killed in following him, and a few more wounded. But whilst he entred at the fore-doore, the enemies despairing of successe, stole out at the back-doore: and taking the benefit of a darke night, escaped the present danger, and recovered their horses: but fled not with such secrecie, but that their flight was quickly knowne, and themselves pursued; the chase being followed at the least sixe miles. But being the night was wondrous darke and the Moone not risen, few of them could be overtaken; so that the businesse ended with the losse of one man onely of Sir John Byron's, and the hurting of fower onely besides himselfe; there being killed some twenty of the Enemies, or thereabouts.[2]

This is easy, rapid narrative; we can follow the action through the dark streets of Burford and emerge again with a distinct idea of what happened. Apart from a few turns of expression, Sir John Berkenhead might be reporting the business *viva voce* to the King. Such prose is not hard to write if you have a story that you really want to tell, and are not hesitating between half a dozen different ways of telling it, or trying to turn it into literature. Signs of hasty writing appear in the phrases "as before was said" and "as was said before"; but the printer is waiting for his copy, and there is no time to make corrections. As Sir John tossed his manuscript to the printer's boy, he might well have echoed the words of the dying Mercutio, "'Tis enough, 'twill serve."

The writers on the parliamentary side were equally convinced of the rightness—indeed, the righteousness—of their cause, and they too were usually driven by a sense of urgency to deliver themselves in direct and highly practical prose. The formidable voice of the Puritan may be heard in the opening sentences of a pamphlet by Richard Overton, published in 1646. The House of Commons, the elected of the people, had imprisoned one of their own number, John Lilburne, who had always been an awkward and independent member, but a determined champion of popular liberties. Overton does not mince his words in his *Remonstrance of Many Thousand Citizens, and other Free-borne People of England, to their owne House of Commons*:

Wee are well assured, yet cannot forget, that the cause of our choosing you to be Parliament-men was to deliver us from all kind of Bondage, and to preserve the Commonwealth in Peace and Happinesse: for effecting whereof, we possessed you with the same Power that was in our selves, to have done the same; for wee might justly have done it our selves without you, if we had thought it convenient, choosing you (as Persons whome wee thought fitly quallified, and Faithfull) for avoiding some inconveniences.

But ye are to remember, this was only of us but a Power of trust (which is ever revokable, and cannot be otherwise), and to be imployed to no other end, than our owne well-being. Nor did wee choose you to continue our Trust's longer, then the knowne established constitution of this Commonly-wealth will justly permit, and that could be but for one yeere at the most: for by our Law, a Parliament is to be called once every yeere, and oftner (if need be), as ye well know. We are your Principalls, and you our Agents; it is a Truth which you cannot but acknowledge: for if you or any other

shall assume, or exercise any Power, that is not derived from our
Trust and choice thereunto, that Power is no lesse than usurpation
and an Oppression, from which wee expect to be freed, in whomso-
ever we finde it; it being altogether inconsistent with the nature of
just Freedome, which yee also very well understand.[3]

This is plain, downright prose; the prose of a man who is
spiritually stripped to the skin. It has no grace or beauty, but
Overton says firmly and unmistakably what he means. It is
prose that comes close to the spoken word (the punctuation
seems to be, in the main, rhetorical), and it has the sort of
tension that results from a writer having a definite reader or
readers in mind. Overton, indeed, is fully conscious of the
glowering and angry opponents to whom his words are addressed; he is a determined David venturing out alone to meet
the parliamentary Goliath.

It would be futile to discuss the prose literature of this period
apart from the events and the spiritual forces which were shap-
ing it. The strong Puritan strain in the English people (at
present in one of its dormant periods) has constantly influenced
English literature, and especially English prose. The same horror
of luxury that drove the Puritans to repudiate and destroy rites
and ceremonies, ecclesiastical vestments and painted windows,
led them also to distrust an ornate prose style,* or indeed any
form of expression that was not the direct and unstudied utterance of strong convictions. As far back as the fourteenth century
we find Wyclif demanding a plain and simple style for preaching; and in the seventeenth century the Puritan insistence on a
bare style, stripped of all decoration and adornment, becomes
more frequent and more emphatic. "All our teaching," says
Richard Baxter in 1656,

must be as Plain and Evident as we can make it. For this doth most
suit to a Teacher's ends. He that would be understood, must speak
to the Capacity of his Hearers, and make it his Business to make
himself understood. Truth loves the Light, and is most Beautiful
when most naked. It is a Sign of an envious Enemy to hide the

*Unless it happened to derive from that of the Bible, in which case it could
be, and often was, highly metaphorical.

Truth; and a Sign of an Hypocrite to do this under pretence of Revealing it: And therefore painted obscure Sermons (like the Painted Glass in the Windows that keep out the Light) are too oft the Marks of painted Hypocrites.[4]

Baxter clearly thinks of "style" as the dress of thought, a dress that conceals the naked truth. His simile of the painted windows shows how naturally his dislike of an elaborate and artificial prose springs from his Puritan distaste for all richness and finery, just as the close-cropped skull of the Roundhead expressed his contempt for the long-haired Cavalier. Many of the Puritans (Baxter himself, for one) were well-educated men; others, such as Bunyan, were self-educated by poring over the Bible and other godly works. But when Baxter states that "he that would be understood must speak to the capacity of his hearers," he has in mind the cobbler and the weaver rather than the Squire and his lady; and this class division goes a long way towards accounting for the plain strength and forthrightness of so much Puritan prose.

The greatest of all the Puritan writers, John Bunyan, habitually spoke to the capacity of his hearers in a prose as bare of ornament as a dissenters' meeting-house, but with a single-minded conviction and a passionate earnestness that made his words shine with an almost unearthly light. "I could have stepped into a style much higher than this in which I have here discoursed," he tells us in the Preface to *Grace Abounding* (1666),

and could have adorned all things more than here I have seemed to do, but I dare not. God did not play in convincing of me, the devil did not play in tempting me, neither did I play when I sunk into a bottomless pit, when the pangs of Hell caught hold upon me; wherefore I may not play in my relating of them, but be plain and simple, and lay down the thing as it was.

To Bunyan, that "chief of sinners" writing down his spiritual autobiography, all style is merely "play"; any sort of writing that is not the immediate utterance of a dedicated soul is frivolous. "The thing as it was" had already been transfigured by the intensity of Bunyan's experience, and could receive no addition from art—or, at any rate, from art as Bunyan conceived it to be. Bunyan's problem as a writer (and it is one that he must have solved almost unconsciously) was how to withdraw his conscious mind from the act of writing, and allow his visions and revelations to find their own words. With Bunyan there was no essential difference between the language of prose and poetry; for everything with him was experience, genuine and important and intensely realized, and everything was expressed in the language of experience.

Such vision, such concentration on the essential, such a complete burning away of all that is irrelevant or adventitious or merely decorative, are to be found perhaps only in Bunyan himself. But the earnestness and directness, the avoidance of all airs and graces and stylistic whimsies, reappear on a rather lower level of intensity in the writings of Baxter, Fox, William Penn, Robert Barclay, and many other less important writers, and such qualities again were to distinguish the prose of Defoe in the politer century that followed.

II

It would be convenient if I could now proceed to draw a sharp contrast between the simplicity of the Puritans and the ornate and elaborate style of their political and religious opponents. But this cannot be done. As the passage quoted from *Mercurius Aulicus* has already indicated, it was not the Puritans only who favoured a direct and simple style of writing. Nor is it only in the practical prose of journalists that we find a preference for unadorned and apparently artless writing: the prose of Izaak Walton, who was writing between 1640 and 1670, is always easy and natural. More remarkable, perhaps, is Thomas Hobbes, who manages to handle abstract subjects with an ease and a dexterity that any writer might envy. When, for example, he writes in his *Leviathan* (1651) of the need to use terms precisely and to examine carefully the definitions given by previous thinkers, he manages, with almost no dilution of his argument, to make his meaning clear to the common reader:

By this it appears how necessary it is for any man that aspires to true Knowledge, to examine the Definitions of former Authors; and either to correct them, where they are negligently set down; or to make them himselfe. For the errours of Definitions multiply themselves, according as the reckoning proceeds; and lead men into absurdities, which at last they see, but cannot avoyd, without reckoning anew from the beginning; in which lyes the foundation of their errours. From whence it happens, that they which trust to books, do as they that cast up many little summs into a greater, without considering whether those little summes were rightly cast up or not; and at last finding the errour visible, and not mistrusting their first grounds, know not which way to cleere themselves; but spend time in fluttering over their bookes; as birds that entring by the chimney, and finding themselves inclosed in a chamber, flutter at the false light of a glasse window, for want of wit to consider which way they came in. So that in the right Definition of Names lyes the first use of Speech; which is the Acquisition of Science: and in the wrong, or no Definitions, lyes the first abuse; from which proceed all false and senselesse Tenets; which make those men that take their instruction from the authority of books, and not from their own meditation, to be as much below the condition of ignorant men, as men endued with true Science are above it. For between true Science, and erroneous Doctrines, Ignorance is in the middle. Naturall sense and imagination are not subject to absurdity. Nature it selfe cannot erre: and as men abound in copiousnesse of language, so they become more wise, or more mad than ordinary.[5]

Thinking was so habitual with Hobbes that his intellectual movements had acquired a sort of natural grace; he had only to set down his own disciplined train of thought to hold the reader's attention. But in actual practice he did much more than that; he took a good deal of trouble, by his illustrations and similes, to make things easy and pleasant for his reader, just as Bernard Shaw, a writer comparable to Hobbes in many ways, exerted himself in the twentieth century to expound political and sociological and scientific ideas to the common reader in a lucid and lively fashion. Both Hobbes and Shaw kept their minds in fine training, and were always ready for any sort of argument; both had a great deal to say, and obviously enjoyed saying it. What we like about them most of all is their verve and their intellectual serenity; and if those qualities go with a sort of jaunty dogmatism (Dryden noticed that Hobbes, like Lucretius, was "everywhere confident of his own reason"[6]), we accept that as the price we must pay for the privilege of conversing with a mind that has almost everything except humility. Stylistically, at any rate, the writing of Hobbes and Shaw, like that of Voltaire or Bertrand Russell, keeps pace with their thought, and has no other function to serve than to convey their ideas to the reader in such a way that he is compelled to look at the ideas and nothing else. Too often we take such writing for granted because it calls so little attention to itself, and reserve our praise for the more pretentious prose of self-conscious stylists.

Although Hobbes, who was born in 1588, was still a hale and vigorous old man in the reign of Charles II, I have mentioned him now because most of his writing was done before the Restoration. But his *Leviathan* was well known to the clever young men who gathered about the court of Charles, and who were soon to exert an unmistakable, and I think fortunate, influence on English prose. What effect Hobbes had on them would be hard to state in precise terms, but I suspect that his lively and temperate prose style was one of his chief attractions. Dryden has puzzled the critics by asserting that if he had any talent for prose it was "owing to his having often read the writings of the great Archbishop Tillotson."[7] Dryden's prose style, indeed, was already formed before Tillotson could have had much influence on him; and with its air of easy but controlled conversation, it comes nearer to that of Hobbes, whom he had certainly read carefully, and whom he must have read (one would have thought) with more enjoyment than he had read the sermons of Tillotson.

It is never safe to claim that anything in literature is new. If I now claim that the Restoration produced a new prose of its own, it will not be difficult to show that everything I am going to call new had been done before. Indeed, I have myself just suggested Hobbes (and I could add several other writers) as a probable influence on Dryden. But there are good reasons for claiming that after 1660 English prose made a fresh start, and that by the end of the century a new style of writing had become general. Much of the credit for the change used to be given to the newly founded Royal Society, whose members were encouraged, as Bishop Sprat tells us, to reject in their writings all "the amplifications, digressions, and swellings of style," and to cultivate "a close, naked, natural way of speaking . . . preferring the language of artizans, countrymen, and merchants, before that of wits and scholars."[8] I certainly do not wish to suggest that the men of the Royal Society had no effect on the prose style of the period; but it is one thing to have a programme, and another to carry it out. Not all of them by any means wrote as well as Sprat, the historian of the Society, or Hooke, its first secretary, and some of them, like Boyle and Evelyn, fell very far short of the expressed ideal. It is perhaps naïve to expect scientists to be much interested in writing; in general, those of them who have been most successful in expounding their subject to the common reader have been looked upon with a certain degree of suspicion by their fellow scientists. In any case, the collective writings of the Restoration men of science were not widely enough known to effect a revolution in prose style.

We shall come nearer to an explanation if we turn our attention to such writers as Dryden and Halifax, and if we give full weight to the fact that Restoration literature was dominated by the aristocracy, who set the tone for it and exercised an unquestioned control over the mode of expression. Restoration prose is, in the main, a slightly formalized variation of the conversation of gentlemen. The gentleman converses with ease, and with an absence of emphasis that may at times become a conscious and studied under-emphasis, but is more often the natural expression of his poise and detachment. He is imperturbable, nothing puts him out or leads him to quicken his pace; indeed, a certain nonchalance and a casual way of making the most devastating remarks are characteristic of him, for if he is always polite he is never mealy-mouthed, and has no middle-class inhibitions. He will never betray too great eagerness or ride his ideas too hard or insist too absolutely, for that is to be a bore; he will not consciously exploit his own personality or indulge in eccentricity or whimsies, for that is to be selfish, to think too much about himself. On all occasions, like a good host, he will consult the convenience and pleasure of those he is entertaining; and he will therefore try to express himself clearly and politely and unpedantically. If he can manage it (and if he can't he won't try) he will make his points with a witty turn of thought and phrase. He will not dogmatize, or proselytize, or appeal exclusively to the emotions; for to do so is the mark of the ignorant zealot and the godly fanatic, of whom no Restoration gentleman wished to be reminded.

Carried into prose, those qualities are characteristic of some of the finest writing of the period. Almost any page of Dryden will show how attractive such prose can be. I choose a passage from a dedication written in 1693:

'Tis a vanity common to all writers, to overvalue their own productions; and 'tis better for me to own this failing in myself, than the world to do it for me. For what other reason have I spent my life in so unprofitable a study? why am I grown old, in seeking so barren a reward as fame? The same parts and application which have made me a poet might have raised me to any honours of the gown, which are often given to men of as little learning and less honesty than myself. No Government has ever been, or ever can be, wherein time-servers and blockheads will not be uppermost. The persons are only changed, but the same jugglings in State, the same hypocrisy in religion, the same self-interest and mismanagement, will remain for ever. Blood and money will be lavished in all ages, only for the preferment of new faces, with old consciences. There is too often a jaundice in the eyes of great men; they see not those whom they raise in the same colours with other men. All whom they affect look golden to them, when the gilding is only in their own distempered sight. These considerations have given me a kind of contempt for those who have risen by unworthy ways. I am not ashamed to be little, when I see them so infamously great; neither do I know why the name of poet should be dishonourable to me, if I am truly one, as I hope I am; for I will never do any thing that shall dishonour it.[9]

Such writing seems so effortless that we may form the impression it is quite unpremeditated. In analysis, however, we shall probably notice some subdued antitheses, and here and there a conscious building up to an unemphatic climax: Dryden may be carried along easily by his thoughts, but he is still controlling them, still finding the right words and the right rhythm to express them. What has almost completely disappeared from his prose is the "periodic" structure, in which the meaning is held in suspense and the structure is not grammatically complete until the close of the sentence. But in compensation for any loss of tension which his looser structure might involve, we find in one sentence after another that the sting is in the tail ("...which are often given to men of as little learning and less honesty than myself"; ". . . only for the preferment of new faces, with old consciences").

The fact that nearly all Dryden's prose writing is in the form of prefaces and dedications should remind us that Restoration prose is not only conversational in tone, but actually is on many occasions a sort of conversation carried on by the writer with some individual, real or imaginary. Where Dryden is not specifically addressing a friend or patron, he still seems to be conscious of a reader. (The preface to *An Evening's Love* begins with the words: "I had thought, Reader, in this Preface . . .") Indeed, the preface, so often a flat and impersonal statement in twentieth-century books, was regularly used by the Restoration author to get on easy terms with his reader, in much the same sort of way as the prologue to a play established a friendly contact between the actors and the audience.

This willingness to "get together" with the reader, and a corresponding unwillingness to write impersonally, or make *ex cathedra* statements, are characteristic of Restoration prose. A pamphleteer, for example, will cast his thoughts into the form of "A Letter from a Gentleman in Town to his Friend in the Country"; and John Eachard puts forth a much longer work, *The Grounds and Occasions of the Contempt of the Clergy*, in the form of a letter to "R. L.," whoever he may be. It is true that Eachard sometimes forgets for fairly long stretches that he is supposed to be writing to "R. L.," but sooner or later he will remember him and maintain the air of familiar discourse by addressing him as "Sir." Again, a surprisingly large amount of Restoration prose is in the form of dialogue. The most famous example is Dryden's *Essay of Dramatic Poesy*, but the dialogue form was used again and again for argument and discussion by such different writers as Boyle in *The Sceptical Chemist*, Simon Patrick in *A Friendly Debate between a Conformist and a Nonconformist*, John Eachard in *Mr. Hobbs's State of Nature Considered*, and Sir Roger L'Estrange in his periodical paper, *The Observator*. On such occasions the writing *must* be conversational, though the conversation may be polite, as in Dryden, or descend to the vulgar idiom in the racy and vigorous journalism of L'Estrange. The popularity of dialogue prose during this period must perhaps be related to the vogue of contemporary comedy; but it is also due to the widespread preference for an informal and familiar mode of expression.

L'Estrange has a special importance here, not only because he was a prolific writer and very widely read, but because he reached a public that was only on the verge of literacy, and that was likely to prefer its authors to write in the simplest terms and in its own colloquial idiom. This public had the time and the inclination to read newspapers; but for the first two decades of Charles II's reign almost no newspapers had been published. The government, acting through the Surveyor of the Press— L'Estrange himself—had effectively suppressed all but its own official journals. In 1679, however, just when the country was at the height of the political crisis precipitated by the Popish Plot, the Press Act expired, and during the next three years a remarkable number of newspapers made their appearance, and were eagerly read. Indeed, the years 1679–1682 are of capital importance in the history of the English newspaper, for it was almost certainly then that the habit of reading newspapers became widespread for the first time. But this same public also learnt to enjoy the political discussion and commentary that it got from such weekly dialogue papers as *Heraclitus Ridens* (1681–2) and L'Estrange's *Observator* (1681–7). L'Estrange, too, carried the very effective dialogue of the *Observator* into some of his political pamphlets. I quote a short snatch from his *Citt and Bumpkin* (1680), in which he exposes the methods by which signatures were obtained to the petitions for a parliament. Bumpkin is unable to understand why, in view of the elaborate organization to secure signatures by fair means or foul, the project was not more successful.

BUMPKIN. But after all this Care and Industry, how was it possible for the Business to Miscarry?

CITT. Why I know 'tis laid in our Dish, that when we had set the whole Kingdom agogg upon *Petitioning*, our hearts would not serve us to go through stitch, and so we drew our necks out of the Collar, and left the Countries in the Lurch.

BUMPKIN. Nay, that's the truth on't, Citt; We stood all gaping for London to lead the way. . . .[10]

With such colloquial expressions as "laid in our dish" and "to go through stitch," L'Estrange keeps in touch with the comparatively uneducated reader. It is true that this is not his only style. He sometimes pitches his appeal a little higher, but his prose never moves very far from the colloquial.

For an example of L'Estrange addressing himself to the more educated public we may turn to the declaration he made in 1663 when he started his *Intelligencer*, published on Mondays, and the *Newes*, published on Thursdays. L'Estrange believed that the country would be quieter and better behaved if there were no newspapers at all, and he took the opportunity of saying so:

I do declare my self, (as I hope I may, in a matter left so absolutely Indifferent, whether Any or None) that supposing the Press in Order; the People in their right Wits, and Newes, or No Newes, to be the Question; A Public Mercury should never have My Vote; because I think it makes the Multitude too Familiar with the Actions, and Counsels of their Superiours, too Pragmaticall and Censorious, and gives them not only an Itch but a kind of Colourable Right, and Licence, to be Meddling with the Government. All which (supposing as before supposed) does not yet hinder, but that in This Juncture, a Paper of That Quality may be both Safe and Expedient: Truly if I should say, Necessary, perhaps the Case would bear it, for certainly, there is not anything, which at This Instant more Imports his Majestie's Service, and the Publick, than to Redeem the

72 ON ENGLISH PROSE

Vulgar from their Former Mistakes, and Delusions, and to preserve
them from the like for the time to come: to both which purposes, the
prudent Manager of a Gazett may Contribute in a very high Degree;
for, beside that 'tis every bodies Money, and (in truth) a good part of
most mens study, and Busness; 'tis none of the worst wayes of Address to the Genius, and Humour of the Common People; whose
Affections are much more capable of being tuned, and wrought
upon, by convenient Hints, and Touches, in the Shape, and Ayre of
a Pamphlet, then by the strongest Reasons, and best Notions imagin-
able, under any other, and more sober Form whatsoever. To which
Advantages of being Popular, and Gratefull, must be added (as none
of the least) that it is likewise seasonable and worth the while, were
there no other use of it, then only to detect, and disappoint the
Malice of those scandalous and false Reports which are daily Contrived, and Bruited against the Government.

So that upon the Mayn, I perceive the Thing Requisite, and (from
ought I can see yet) Once a week may do the bus'ness, (for I intend
to utter my News, by Weight, and not by Measure). Yet if I shall
find, when my hand is In, and after the planting, and securing of
my Correspondents, that the Matter will fairly furnish More, without
either Incertainty, Repetition, or Impertinence, I shall keep my self
free to double at pleasure. . . .[11]

L'Estrange has taken some care in setting forth this statement
of policy; yet, if he avoids the more vulgar and proverbial idiom
that he was later to use in The Observator, the writing is
noticeably casual and familiar, and in such phrases as "it is
everybody's money," "once a week may do the business," and
"when my hand is in" the conversational tone is unmistakable.
In relating the news in his "public mercury" L'Estrange adopted
an easy narrative style, and he was followed in this by most of
his journalistic successors in the seventeenth and early eighteenth
centuries. In view of the extent to which English prose was
corrupted in the nineteenth century by the pompous phraseology
of newspaper writers, we have no right to assume that the
journalist will always throw his influence on the side of easy and
natural expression. English prose, however, owes a good deal
to L'Estrange and his immediate contemporaries and successors
who gave the Englishman his daily news—and the news, after

all, was his main reason for reading at all—in a lively and straightforward style.

When, as occasionally happened, L'Estrange was moved to indignation, his more elaborate periods still retained the movement of speech; he was still consciously addressing a reader, pleading with him, or exhorting him, or bullying him—never unaware of his presence. I quote from *The Reformed Catholique* (1679), where L'Estrange is attacking the Scots:

The Story of these Phantastical Conspiracies is almost as Nauseous as the thing it self is Detestable; only this last in Scotland methinks seems to Crown the Infamy of all the rest. For a Party that calls it self Protestant; a Party in full Cry upon the scent of Popery; a Popish Plot upon Oath too, at the same time upon the Life of the King, upon the Life of our King, upon our Religion and Government; and that Plot, at that Instant under a strict Examination; the same Party at the same time also pressing for Justice upon the Conspirators, nay, and complaining of the remissness of the Prosecution, notwithstanding the most exemplary Rigor in the Case that ever was known in this Nation: for this party, (I say) under these Circumstances, to flie in the face of the Government, let the World judge if ever there was a more Consummated piece of Wickedness. They raise a Rebellion, and make Religion the Ground of it; they declare a War against the King, and the Church, and yet write themselves Loyal Subjects and Protestants. . . .[12]

This last passage ought to remind us of another and more famous writer. The loose colloquial piling-up of a climax, together with the syntactical impasse ("for this party (I say) . . . let the world judge if ever there was . . .") in which L'Estrange lands himself, are characteristic of Defoe.* Politically the two men may have been poles apart, but their literary situation was

*Defoe's style probably owed a good deal to his reading of L'Estrange. It is interesting to find that William Lee, who lists a number of Defoe's favourite expressions ("scarcely any of them similarly used by any other writer of that age"), begins his list with "let the World know" and "I say." (William Lee, *Daniel Defoe: His Life and Hitherto Unknown Writings* [1869], I.vi.) Defoe's habit, in *The Review* and elsewhere, of addressing his readers as "Gentlemen" might have been caught from L'Estrange. Cf. *The Intelligencer*, 7 September, 1663: "I do not doubt, Gentlemen, but you have heard of the late Rising in Ireland. . . ."

similar: both wrote fluently for an expectant printer, and neither had much time for the niceties of construction. Circumstances such as these may lead to chaotic writing, but there is little of that in either L'Estrange or Defoe; both men were carried to a successful conclusion by the strong impetus of their thought, and by a reassuring absence of all anxiety about correctness. "Nor shall I give myself much pain about the style," L'Estrange tells his reader, "but let it e'en prove as it hits and lye as it falls. . . ."[13] Defoe is equally self-possessed:

Let not those Gentlemen who are Criticks in Stile, in Method or Manner, be angry that I have never pull'd off my Cap to them in Humble Excuse for my loose Way of treating the World as to Language, Expression, and Politeness of Phrase; Matters of this Nature differ from most things a Man can write: When I am busied writing Essays, and Matters of Science, I shall address them for their Aid, and take as much Care to avoid their Displeasure as becomes me; but when I am upon the Subject of Trade and the Variety of Casual Story, I think my self a little loose from the Bonds of Cadence and Perfections of Stile, and satisfie my self in my Study to be explicit, easie, free, and very plain; and for all the rest, *Nec Careo, nec Curo.*[14]

From almost every quarter, then, a reaction had set in against the elaborate periods and the learned vocabulary of Milton, Browne, and Jeremy Taylor. The Anglican pulpit held out for some time, but the same movement towards a less artificial and more conversational style becomes apparent in the sermons of South and Tillotson. In the aristocratic culture of Restoration London, the scholar was now in comparatively low repute, at any rate as a writer; and we find even Dryden, a Westminster boy and a Cambridge man, writing contemptuously of the lazy gownsmen, and remarking upon the need to rub off the rust acquired at the universities.[15] Looking back on this period from the standpoint of the mid-eighteenth century, David Hume observed that the separation of the learned from what he called the "conversible" world must have had "a very bad influence both on books and company."[16] Whether the separation was as absolute as Hume supposed, it is clear that to the fine gentleman of the Restoration a little learning was a dangerous thing, and a lot of learning was fatal. Erudition, too much conversing with books, too much studious retirement, led to pedantry; and pedantry was a sort of intellectual body-odour. It is not therefore surprising to find some of the scholars attempting to give a modish turn to their writing. But if John Eachard and Walter Pope managed to carry their learning lightly, and even amusingly, Jeremy Collier's sallies are not always so happy, and Thomas Rymer has the sad gaiety of a dancing bear.

III

In the prose of Addison and Steele, of Swift and Arbuthnot and Mandeville, the same tradition of easy and polite writing persists. By choice or circumstance, the greater part of what they wrote took the form of the author addressing himself directly to the reader: Isaac Bickerstaff, Mr. Spectator, Lemuel Gulliver, the imaginary projector in *A Modest Proposal*, and so on, are all writing in the first person. It would be quite untrue to say that good prose has never been written except by an author who has managed to establish this sort of personal contact with the reader; but the consciousness of a reader, real or imaginary, acts as a continual discipline to the writer. It encourages him, as we have seen, to discourse amiably and politely, it makes pedantry and self-indulgence of all kinds almost impossible, and it keeps the tone lively. The eighteenth-century author succeeded to a remarkable degree in writing personally without thrusting his personality upon the reader. He did this either by adopting a mask (Mr. Spectator, Lemuel Gulliver, Captain Hercules Vinegar, the Rambler), or by exercising a natural or acquired restraint which kept him from insisting too much on his own personality when he appeared in public. In reading Henry Fielding, for example, we are always conscious of the author being there in person, but he is there as a master of ceremonies, and not as an exhibitionist. It is true that we do not find much of this self-effacement in Defoe; but if, when reading him, we are more than usually conscious of the urgent voice appealing to us or arguing with us, it is not because he is parading his personality, but because he has a good deal less of the conventional restraint and politeness of his century. In the middle-class Defoe there is still a distinct strain of the old Puritan preacher, so that we often get the impression that his prose is not addressed so much to the solitary reader as to an audience of listeners. On every other page of the *Review*, and even in many of his pamphlets, he has the habit of bringing us into the discussion; it is the technique of the speaker, exclamatory, emphatic, earnest, and familiar.

Not all the contemporaries of Addison and Swift and Defoe had mastered this familiar and conversational style. In the writing of such scholars as Richard Bentley and William Warburton we often find ourselves floundering in ponderous sentences, and stunned by a learned and polysyllabic vocabulary. But in the first half of the eighteenth century the new familiar and friendly prose was firmly established as the accepted mode, and there is little writing in that period which is not easy and unassuming. It is significant, too, that this colloquial ease is not confined to the familiar essay or letter, but is to be found in the philosophers —in Locke and Shaftesbury, in Berkeley and Hume—and, with some exceptions, in the historians, theologians, and men of science. The liaison between the learned and the conversible worlds was almost complete. The standards were still aristocratic; and, because they were so, prose had the well-bred freedom that is one of the natural accompaniments of confident aristocracy. When the centre of gravity shifts in the nineteenth century to the middle class, a new gentility—the mark of social uncertainty —begins to make itself felt. It is significant to find John Addington Symonds, writing in 1890, remarking on the uninhibited prose of the previous century. "Few men of letters nowadays," he observes, "would dare to follow Swift and Sterne, those classics of our prose, in their bold use of colloquialisms."[17]

I have called the period stretching from 1660 to 1800 the Age of Prose, for it seems to me that during those years English prose was constantly doing its natural work of appealing to the intelligence of the common reader. At no other period has the general level of writing been so high, or the limitations of prose communication better understood. When we wish to give high praise to a poem we can say quite naturally that it is "great poetry." When we think highly of a piece of prose writing, we are more likely to say "This is good prose." Whenever I hear the expression "great prose" or "fine prose" I am apt to suspect that it is something which I should not greatly care to read: a purple passage from De Quincey, perhaps, or from Ruskin, or from Doughty's *Travels in Arabia Deserta*. I am quite willing to call Swift a great prose writer, so long as it is agreed that what he gives us—with an astonishing consistency—is good prose. Every Sunday when he went to church Swift had the chance of listening to a kind of prose that exists on a higher level of utterance than he ever attempted:

In the year that King Uzziah died I saw also the Lord sitting upon a throne, high and lifted up, and his train filled the temple.

Above it stood the seraphims: each one had six wings; with twain he covered his face, with twain he covered his feet, and with twain he did fly.

If that passage is really prose, I shall have to call it great prose; but this vision of the prophet Isaiah, itself so "high and lifted up," is surely poetry. Prose, it is true, touches on poetry at one extreme, and on pure scientific communication at the other; but at its most characteristic it occupies a wide field of humane discourse and intelligent discussion. It is good prose when it allows the writer's meaning to come through with the least possible loss of significance and nuance, as a landscape is seen through a clear window. Something very near to this was achieved by many eighteenth-century writers, and notably by Swift. We can read page after page of Swift, absorbing the ideas completely and continuously, and scarcely conscious of the author. Scarcely conscious, but never quite unaware of him: Swift still has his own unmistakable voice, and no good prose has the transparency or anonymity of a window-pane. What it is that we recognize when we say, "That is Swift," would be hard to define; but I

suspect that in the final analysis what is most personal to a prose
writer is an individual rhythm, a rhythm of both thought and
language.

IV

The prose style we have been considering was too good to
last. It is not the style favoured by most of the writers of the
later eighteenth century—by Johnson, or Gibbon, or Sir Joshua
Reynolds, or Burke. With those writers we return, in varying
degrees, to the more formal and balanced periods of the seventeenth century, and, with some of them at least, to a vocabulary
more characteristic of the scholar than the man of the world.
How far the influence of Johnson was responsible for setting
a new fashion in writing it would be difficult to tell; but his
Rambler essays were widely read in book form, and they must
have had a considerable effect on his younger contemporaries.[18]
Johnson's style was the natural expression of a confident mind
and an emphatic personality, of a man accustomed to ordering
his thoughts and making critical decisions. His air of finality is
partly the result of moral and intellectual certitude. But it may
also have resulted from a conscious effort to enforce his ideas
on the mind of the reader. In discussing the prose of Swift, he
remarks on the ease and simplicity with which Swift habitually
expressed his ideas, and yet he is unwilling to give him unquali-
fied praise:

This easy and safe conveyance of meaning it was Swift's desire to
attain, and for having attained it he deserves praise, though perhaps
not the highest praise. For purposes merely didactick, when something is to be told that was not known before, it is the best mode;
but against that inattention by which known truths are suffered to
lie neglected it makes no provision; it instructs, but does not
persuade.[19]

In making this distinction Johnson has returned, in so many
words, to Bacon's contrast between the kind of prose which
records, or states, or reports, or conveys ideas cleanly and precisely, and that very different kind of writing which Bacon called

"magistral and peremptory," and which aims at persuasion, at inducing belief.

In accounting for the shift that was taking place in the second half of the eighteenth century from a familiar to a more artificial and rhetorical style, we should perhaps give some weight to the influence of the Scottish writers. Some of those were eminent men, such as William Robertson the historian and Adam Smith the political economist; and at a lower level there were many Scotsmen, then as now, running the newspapers, writing articles for monthly periodicals, or working as compilers and translators and hack-writers for the booksellers. The literary Scot was in a peculiar position. Although he was probably better educated than most of his English contemporaries, he was linguistically at a disadvantage, for he spoke one language and wrote another. An educated Scot could, of course, make himself fairly well understood in London; but the difference in the spoken language on the two sides of the Border was much more marked than it is today. Quite apart from some odd words in his vocabulary, and of course his pronunciation, the Scot did not speak idiomatic English, and he knew it. When, therefore, he came before the public as a writer, he naturally tended to throw his sentences into an elaborate and artificial form, and to employ a vocabulary that was more literary than colloquial. The kind of prose that was normally beyond his powers was the easy idiomatic discourse of Addison and Swift, which, as I have suggested, was a development from the conversation of English gentlemen. The Scot could not risk using a familiar and idiomatic phraseology, not because he was not a gentleman, but because he was not an English one. It is not therefore surprising to find Burke saying of Robertson that he wrote like a man "who composes in a dead language which he understands but cannot speak."[20] One might have expected Irishmen to suffer from the same disability, but in fact the speech of the Irish and the English was much more alike than that of the English and the Scots. Unless one knew that Goldsmith was an Irishman one would be unlikely to guess it from his prose style; but Smollett and Hugh Blair and Robertson and Adam Smith, and even at times the travelled Boswell, all betrayed the country of their origin, and no doubt helped considerably to establish the more elaborate and less idiomatic prose that became so common in the later eighteenth century.

Whatever the cause may have been, the change is apparent enough. It is a change not only from the natural to the artificial, and from the simple to the elegant, but, as I have already suggested, from the aristocratic to the genteel. No doubt it is part of a larger social change which could be traced in public manners, in dress, in architecture and furniture, in the drama and fiction of the period, and in much else. In prose the effect can be deplorable. In 1769, for example, a certain Edward Harwood, D.D., published a work to which he gave the title, *A Liberal Translation of the New Testament: Being an Attempt to translate the Sacred Writings with the same Freedom, Spirit, and Elegance, With which other English Translations of the Greek Classics have lately been executed.* . . . Impressed by the style of Johnson, Robertson, Bishop Lowth, and other modern authors, Harwood wished, as he put it, to clothe the scriptures "in the vest of modern elegance." The result of his labours may be seen in 1 Corinthians, xiii. In the Authorized Version verses 4–6 read:

Charity suffereth long and is kind: charity envieth not, charity vaunteth not itself, is not puffed up.

Doth not behave itself unseemly, seeketh not her own, is not easily provoked, thinketh no evil.

Rejoiceth not in iniquity, but rejoiceth in the truth.

Clothed in the vest of modern elegance this becomes, in Harwood's translation:

Benevolence is unruffled, is benign: Benevolence cherishes no ambitious desires: Benevolence is not ostentatious, is not inflated with insolence.

It preserves a consistent decorum; is not enslaved to sordid interest; is not transported with furious passion; indulges no malevolent design.

It conceives no delight from the perpetration of wickedness; but is the first to applaud truth and virtue.

It throws a veil of candour over all things.

Or here is Harwood dealing with the miracle of the loaves and fishes. Where the Authorized Version tells us that Jesus "commanded them to make all sit down by companies upon the green grass," Harwood has this:

He then ordered his disciples to desire the multitude to digest themselves into regular companies, and to sit down on the verdant turf.[21]

If Harwood carried things to an extreme, he is still symptomatic of what was happening to English prose. The same debilitating process may be seen at work in such a third-rate writer as Laetitia-Matilda Hawkins. This lady, the daughter of Johnson's friend, Sir John Hawkins, a man who had risen in the world, published two volumes of *Memoirs* in 1824. (The hyphenated Laetitia-Matilda is perhaps a small indication of this lady's determination to consolidate the social ground her father had gained.) On every page of her memoirs we meet with a sort of simpering gentility that is no doubt an expression of her own character, but is also typical of a new middle-class refinement:

My younger brother remembers to have met Mrs. Paradise one day at dinner at Mrs. Welch's; her personal attractions were at that time much on the decline, and her countenance retained little other expression but that of extreme irritability. She then resided at one of the villages in the neighbourhood of London, and regretting that there was no stage-coach from her village, which would convey her to that part of London to which her business occasionally called her, he suggested that the deficiency might be supplied by availing herself of another conveyance, to take her to her place of destination, when she quitted the stage. Upon which, turning to him, with a most emphatical look and tone of voice, she said, "Lord! Sir, you might as well advise me to cut off my nose to improve my face." My brother was astonished, and could not perceive any connection between the two propositions.[22]

When people have to have countenances and to reside in villages, when they do not take a coach but avail themselves of a conveyance, we have moved a long way from the prose of Swift, and still further from that of Defoe. "Never use a short word when a long one is available" seems to have been the principle on which writers like Harwood and Miss Hawkins proceeded; and as we enter the nineteenth century we shall find that it was a principle only too often followed—or, as Dr. Harwood might have said, a principle which was made the object of too frequent observation and too assiduous cultivation.

IV. THE NINETEENTH CENTURY
AND AFTER

NOW THAT WE HAVE come half way through the twentieth century, we can look back at the nineteenth and see it as a distinct historical period. Already the literary scholars are busy assessing the great Victorian writers, publishing their letters, and editing their works. No one, however, has yet written a history of nineteenth-century English prose. The subject is at once too vast and too various, and still too close to us to make it easy for the critic to disengage those qualities that are peculiar to nineteenth-century prose writers.* There is always a time-lag in literary, as in other, fashions; the prose style of the later eighteenth century survived, with some loss of elegance, well into the nineteenth, and characteristic features of nineteenth-century prose still survive today in the editorials of the less modern newspapers, and in the writing of those authors, whether academic or not, whose minds turn naturally to the past. Yet although the stages of development are by no means clear-cut, certain general influences have been at work, and it is not difficult to see some of the results.

Of those influences the most important has been the steady growth of the reading public. When he reviewed Crabbe's *Tales* in 1812 for the *Edinburgh Review*, Francis Jeffrey estimated that there were "probably not less than 200,000 persons who read for amusement or instruction, among the middling classes of

---

*For the sake of convenience I stick to the usual literary divisions of "eighteenth century" and "nineteenth century," without of course wishing to suggest that any startling change was to be expected merely because one century had ended in 1800 and another had begun in 1801.

society, and rather fewer than 20,000 in the higher classes."[1] Thirty-three years later, when he was making a selection of his reviews for publication in book form, he either decided that he had underestimated the size of the reading public, or—what is more probable—was convinced that it had increased very considerably in the interval, for he amended the original figures to 300,000 and 30,000. Such estimates, of course, are only informed guesses; but as editor of the *Edinburgh* Jeffrey was perhaps as likely as anyone to know the facts about the literary world of the early nineteenth century. In making his estimate he was concerned only with the readers of what used to be called "polite literature": the number of those who could read, and did read, newspapers and other ephemeral literature must have been very much larger. At any rate, if Jeffrey's figures can be accepted, they point to a larger public of middle-class readers than had existed a hundred years earlier; and the remarkable sale of Scott's poems and novels, and of the poems of Crabbe and Byron, would seem to confirm his estimate. We can certainly say that the potential public for Macaulay's *History of England* in 1849 was much more numerous than that for Hume's *History of England* almost a century earlier, and the great majority of Macaulay's readers must have been drawn from the well-to-do middle class. In the eighteenth century a much larger proportion of them would have belonged to the upper class. That, at least, was how Wordsworth sized up the situation in the last decade of that century. Reflecting in his *Prelude* that it is the people who can afford to *buy* books who really determine what shall be written, and how it shall be written, Wordsworth complained

> How books mislead us, seeking their reward
> From judgments of the wealthy few. . . .[2]

By 1850 the "wealthy few" were not nearly so few, and the steady growth of circulating libraries (though these usually required a subscription) had made it much less necessary for the reader of a book to be also the purchaser. The new readers were the families—and Victorian parents were normally prolific —of rich industrialists and well-to-do merchants and shopkeepers, with perhaps a distinct preponderance of female over male readers.

It would be a crude simplification to suggest that Scott and Charlotte Brontë, Dickens and Thackeray and George Eliot, Carlyle and Macaulay, Ruskin and Matthew Arnold, merely gave the public the sort of prose that it wanted; but it would be to ignore the evidence to deny that all of these writers were, in their own way, fully conscious of the reading public, and that it had a considerable influence on their style of writing. The situation in the present century is rather different. The potential public is now so vast that no writer today thinks of reaching the whole of it. The nearest we now get to anything approaching a universal appeal is in a broadcast talk made to the nation in a moment of crisis, and even that is rarely effective on all levels at once. Knowing that he cannot hope to interest, or even make himself fully intelligible to, the whole of the contemporary reading public, the twentieth-century novelist or historian does not even try: he writes for his own public, whatever that may be. The chances are that his public will be people more or less like himself, with a comparable range of interests and a similar outlook on life. Some such restriction may have been forced upon the twentieth-century author; but if, as often happens with the sensitive and intelligent young writer, he consciously addresses himself to some sort of Third Programme public, he is in danger of being led into preciosity and obscurity and a cult of the esoteric.

The Victorian writer, on the other hand, seems to have made a manly attempt—at least up to the last quarter of the century—to write for the common reader. The readers of Dickens may not have been so representative of the whole of the English people as the first audiences of Shakespeare's plays, but a novel by Dickens, like a play of Shakespeare's, appealed to men and women of widely different social and intellectual levels. The Victorian novel has therefore breadth and sanity and variety; and if it is written in a style that may at times be slightly above the heads of the humblest readers, it is on the whole universally intelligible. Yet this wide general appeal is not gained without some loss. Victorian prose is rarely subtle; it is more likely to be confidently emphatic and comfortably self-possessed, and it is at its most characteristic the voice of omniscience addressing ignorance.

This robust and assured prose antedates the Victorian age. We can meet with it on almost any page of the *Edinburgh Review*, and it reverberates with indomitable assurance in the literary voice of the editor himself. In 1825, more than a decade before the young Queen came to the throne, Jeffrey was reviewing a translation into English of Goethe's *Wilhelm Meister's Apprenticeship*. He noted the high reputation of Goethe's work in Germany, and then advanced to the attack on a broad front:

We must say, then, at once, that we cannot enter into the spirit of this German idolatry; nor at all comprehend upon what grounds the work before us could ever be considered as an admirable, or even a commendable performance. To us it certainly appears, after the most deliberate consideration, to be eminently absurd, puerile, incongruous, vulgar, and affected; and, though redeemed by considerable powers of invention, and some traits of vivacity, to be so far from perfection, as to be, almost from beginning to end, one flagrant offence against every principle of taste, and every just rule of composition. Though indicating, in many places, a mind capable both of acute and profound reflection, it is full of mere silliness and childish affectation; and though evidently the work of one who had seen and observed much, it is throughout altogether unnatural, and not so properly improbable, as affectedly fantastical and absurd—kept, as it were, studiously aloof from general or ordinary nature—never once bringing us into contact with real life or genuine character—and, where not occupied with the professional squabbles, paltry jargon, and scenical profligacy of strolling players, tumblers, and mummers (which may be said to form its staple) is conversant only with incomprehensible mystics and vulgar men of whim, with whom, if it were at all possible to understand them, it would be a baseness to be acquainted. . . .³

What strikes one first and most forcibly in this passage is Jeffrey's utter confidence in his own judgment, a confidence that is reflected in his positive assertions, and in the rounded and controlled rhythm of his sentences. When a man like Jeffrey says

"We cannot at all comprehend" or "We are at a loss to understand," he manages to convey the impression that the failure is not at all to be laid to his account, but to that of the writer he is examining. So sure is Jeffrey of himself that his sentences frequently move to a deliberate climax, and the climax is one of his devices for putting pressure on the reader's judgment. The same purpose is served by his passages of contempt (expressed here in the various derogatory epithets he uses, e.g., "absurd," "puerile," "vulgar," "paltry"), and by his pharisaic distaste for "strolling players, tumblers, and mummers," and those "vulgar men of whim, with whom . . . it would be a baseness to be acquainted." Jeffrey comes before us as the man of taste condemning the literary law-breaker, and taking exception to anything that is not refined ("vulgar" and "absurd" both occur twice in this short passage) and not adult ("puerile," "childish"). The whole passage has a judicial air, and we are reminded that in addition to being an editor and literary critic, Jeffrey was also a judge in the Scottish Court of Session. But the judicial impartiality is more apparent than real. Such phrases as "though redeemed by considerable powers of invention," and "though indicating, in many places, a mind capable both of acute and profound reflection," are little more than rhetorical devices to give the reader the impression that the critic is being scrupulously fair; in reality, they are so many jumping-off points for a further attack—it is a case of *reculer pour mieux sauter*. Again, Jeffrey *seems* to be appealing to the reader's intelligence, and to be examining all the evidence fairly before offering judgment; but in fact he is not so much the impartial judge as the prosecuting counsel, whose aim is to persuade the jury to accept his case rather than to encourage them to reach a decision of their own.

This, then, is the big bow-wow manner of the monthly reviewer, the style of the orator rather than the conversationalist; and the *Edinburgh* was, after all, a sort of public platform from which the editor and his contributors addressed the nation. Jeffrey's style of writing is a variation of the old Ciceronian prose; and it represents fairly enough the manner of those numerous nineteenth-century authors who convey instruction firmly and forcibly, but always at the risk of stunning their reader into a state of dazed acquiescence. The reader is left in no doubt about what he is to think, but the thinking has been done for him; the issues have been settled, the matter is closed.

This authoritative air persists in much Victorian writing; in the prose of Macaulay, of course, but also in the work of so different a writer as Matthew Arnold. Arnold was essentially an educator; and when he sat down to write such a book as *Culture and Anarchy* he had already visualized his readers as some sort of adult class to be instructed—a class of pupils not incapable of responding to reason, but wrong-headed and not particularly bright and very much at the mercy of their Victorian environment. All that being so, they had to have things put to them plainly and hammered home with a good deal of repetition. The effect of Arnold's dialectic is sometimes monotonous, but at other times—when, for instance, he is addressing an Oxford audience —it can be brilliant.

He is at his tantalizing best in a well-known passage in which he deflates the prosperous complacency of Sir Charles Adderley and Mr. Roebuck. He begins by citing a newspaper report of one of Sir Charles Adderley's speeches to the Warwickshire farmers. (Adderley, a wealthy Warwickshire landowner, sat as a Tory member of parliament for the northern division of Staffordshire.)

"Talk of the improvement of breed! Why, the race we ourselves represent, the men and women, the old Anglo-Saxon race, are the best breed in the whole world. . . . The absence of a too enervating climate, too unclouded skies, and a too luxurious nature, has produced so vigorous a race of people, and has rendered us so superior to all the world."

Arnold now turns to a comparable burst of oratory from Mr. Roebuck addressing his constituents in Sheffield*:

"I look around me and ask what is the state of England? Is not property safe? Is not every man able to say what he likes? Can you

---

*John Arthur Roebuck (1801–1879), M.P. for Sheffield, described in D.N.B. as "short in stature, vehement in speech, bold in opinion." He "addressed popular audiences with easy assurance and great effect."

not walk from one end of England to the other in perfect security? I ask you whether, the world over or in past history, there is anything like it? Nothing. I pray that our unrivalled happiness may last.

After some critical comments in a subdued key, Arnold suddenly produces his third newspaper clipping, which he says he happened to stumble upon immediately after reading the report of Mr. Roebuck's speech:

"A shocking child murder has just been committed at Nottingham. A girl named Wragg left the workhouse there on Saturday morning with her young illegitimate child. The child was soon afterwards found dead on Mapperly Hills, having been strangled. Wragg is in custody."[4]

From those three motifs Arnold now proceeds to compose his critical symphony. "Nothing but that," he begins, looking back at the last of his three extracts,

but, in juxtaposition with the absolute eulogies of Sir Charles Adderley and Mr. Roebuck, how eloquent, how suggestive are those few lines! "Our old Anglo-Saxon breed, the best in the whole world!" —how much that is harsh and ill-favoured there is in this best! *Wragg!* If we are to talk of ideal perfection, of "the best in the whole world," has anyone reflected what a touch of grossness in our race, what an original shortcoming in the more delicate spiritual perceptions, is shown by the natural growth amongst us of such hideous names—Higginbottom, Stiggins, Bugg! In Ionia and Attica they were luckier in this respect than "the best race in the world"; by the Ilissus there was no Wragg, poor thing! And "our unrivalled happiness"— what an element of grimness, bareness, and hideousness mixes with it and blurs it; the workhouse, the dismal Mapperly Hills—how dismal those who have seen them will remember—the gloom, the smoke, the cold, the strangled illegitimate child! "I ask you whether, the world over or in past history, there is anything like it?" Perhaps not, one is inclined to answer; but at any rate, in that case, the world is very much to be pitied. And the final touch—short, bleak and inhuman: *Wragg is in custody.* The sex lost in the confusion of our unrivalled happiness; or (shall I say?) the superfluous Christian name lopped off by the straightforward vigour of our old Anglo-Saxon breed! There is profit for the spirit in such contrasts as this; criticism serves the cause of perfection by establishing them. . . .[5]

If Arnold had been replying to a speech of Sir Charles Adderley in the Oxford Union, he could hardly have made a more telling use of the words of his opponent. The sardonic repetition of "the best race in the world," "our unrivalled happiness," and the rest, is effected without monotony, and indeed with considerable wit. With each repetition, the phrase in its new context appears less and less justifiable, more and more silly. Arnold's words had, in fact, been written to be spoken; they form part of a lecture delivered from the Chair of Poetry at Oxford on 29 October, 1864. The ridicule, the sardonic asides, the pompous phrases held up for our cynical inspection, the tone of restrained familiarity, all suggest the lecturer and—on this occasion, at least—seem to invite cultured manifestations of laughter and applause. But Arnold carried this lecturing style into his ordinary prose writing; so much of his prose is polemical, consciously directed against the Philistines, that his lecturing manner was almost forced upon him. His usual audience was not quite the Philistines themselves, but some sort of middle-class intelligentsia, no doubt a good deal more Philistine than Arnold himself, and certainly less finicky, but willing to listen to so impressive an expert on culture. Arnold's repetitions, however, are not always so subtly managed as they are in the Wragg passage. Too often he is content with mere reiteration, as in his tedious playing upon the phrase "Scotch drink, Scotch religion, and Scotch manners" when he is labouring the point that Burns did not come from the same cultural environment as Dante.[6] On such occasions the voice we hear is that of the schoolmaster drilling a dull class.

Though the pedagogical tone is more marked in Arnold than in most of his contemporaries, it is certainly one of the dominant notes in Victorian prose, and it can hardly be disassociated from the large and growing public of new middle-class readers, willing to be taught by their betters, and eager to absorb facts and opinions. If the teacher is to retain his authority over the class, he must be able to give the impression that he always knows the answer, that he is never in any doubt himself. With the very best boys he can perhaps afford to drop the mask and raise questions that he cannot answer, or explore territory that lies beyond the known and the certain; but such spiritual adventures are only for the few, since it is only the few who are fit. For the most part the Victorian writer remains unquestionably superior to his readers; if not omniscient, he is at any rate authoritative, self-assured, at times a little condescending, but nearly always willing to make himself generally understood. What we may miss in nineteenth-century prose is more writing with the distinction of Cardinal Newman's; but Newman took the sort of trouble over everything he wrote that few of his Victorian contemporaries were prepared to take. With such a large and, on the whole, undiscriminating reading public, the temptation to take things too easily must have been almost irresistible.

Something of this sort seems to have happened with Charles Dickens, who knew his public as an actor knows his audience. It is dangerous to take Dickens as being representative of any kind of writing but his own; he was very much of an individualist, and it is perhaps only in that respect that he can be called characteristic of the Victorian writer. Yet one feature of his style, amounting almost to a mannerism, has some affinities with the repetition that we have been considering in Matthew Arnold. Dickens constantly employed repetition for the sake of emphasis, and for humorous and emotional effects of one sort or another; but the repeating of words and phrases is so much an integral part of his normal prose style as to suggest that it also had the humble function of making his writing easy to read by the widest possible public. A passage from *Our Mutual Friend* will serve to show how gradually, and with what a circular movement, Dickens imparts information to his readers:

Mr. Podsnap's *world* was not a very large *world*, morally; no, nor even geographically: seeing that although his business was sustained upon commerce with *other countries*, he considered *other countries*, with that important reservation, a mistake, and of their manners and customs would conclusively observe, "Not English!" when PRESTO! with a flourish of the arm, and a flush of the face, they were swept away. Elsewise, the world *got up at eight, shaved close at a quarter past, breakfasted at nine, went to the City at ten, came home at half-past five, and dined at seven.* Mr. Podsnap's notions of the Arts in their integrity might have been stated thus. Literature; large print, respectively descriptive of *getting up at eight, shaving close at a quarter past, breakfasting at nine, going to the City at ten, coming home at half-past five, and dining at seven.* Painting and sculpture; models and portraits representing Professors of *getting up at eight, shaving close at a quarter past, breakfasting at nine, going to the City at ten, coming home at half-past five, and dining at seven.* Music; a respectable performance (without variations) on stringed and wind instruments, sedately expressive of *getting up at eight, shaving close at a quarter past, breakfasting at nine, going to the City at ten, coming home at half-past five, and dining at seven. Nothing else* to be permitted to those same vagrants the Arts, on pain of excommunication. *Nothing else* To Be—anywhere!

As a so eminently respectable man, Mr. Podsnap was sensible of its being required of him to take *Providence* under his protection. Consequently he always knew exactly *what Providence meant.* Inferior and less respectable men might fall short of that mark, but Mr. Podsnap was always up to it. And it was very remarkable (and must have been very comfortable) that *what Providence meant,* was invariably *what Mr. Podsnap meant.* . . .

The Podsnaps lived in *a shady angle* adjoining Portman Square. They were a kind of people certain to dwell in the *shade,* wherever they dwelt. Miss Podsnap's life had been, from her first appearance on this planet, altogether *of a shady order;* for Mr. Podsnap's *young person* was likely to get little good out of association with *other young persons,* and had therefore been restricted to companionship with not very congenial *older persons,* and with massive furniture. . . .[7]

By italicizing the words and phrases that Dickens has repeated, I have, of course, given them a false prominence. Most of them are not intended to be emphatic, and when we have made due allowance for the humorous intention, I think we must conclude that the main purpose of the constant repetition is to lead the reader easily from one stage to another, so that when he is being asked to absorb something new, he has also got something familiar to give him encouragement. Dickens continually goes back on his tracks in this way, progressing in a gradual movement that gives the reader plenty of time to keep pace with him. His repetitive style, then, is an aid to reading, and must be associated with a reading public so large, and on its outer fringes so inexpert, that things had to be made easy for it.

In the prose of Jeffrey we found confidence, the voice of authority. But Jeffrey is characteristic of the nineteenth century in another way: he is fluent, but the fluency becomes at times too facile; he commands a large vocabulary, and he is never at a loss, but ultimately we begin to feel that his is the sort of prose that is written by a man who has to fill too many pages too frequently. One of the clues to an understanding of the Victorian age is its love of amplitude. The houses were large, the pictures on the walls were large; even the dishes and spoons and cruet-stands were, by our scales, Brobdingnagian. In a century in which amplitude was a guarantee of solid achievement, in which size was equated with prosperity, literature was large too. It was an age of long poems and three-volume novels, of extensive histories and elephantine biographies and interminable book reviews. The words flowed on in a broad river, and inevitably there was much pompous and undistinguished writing. We find Victorian prose at its most flatulent in the newspapers, the monthly reviews, and the decorous biographies of Victorian worthies, where the writer has too little to say and all the room in the world to say it. The great Victorian novelists, on the other hand, had a lot that they wanted to say, and they usually managed to say it simply. Thomas Hardy, oddly enough, is something of an exception. Although he could write dialogue that has the ring of complete authenticity, he has also the fondness of the self-educated man for grandiose expressions, and seems determined at times to show his readers that he is as well educated as the best of them.

Although the time of bare boughs had now set in there were sheltered hollows amid the Hintock plantations and copses in which a more tardy leave-taking than on windy summits was the rule with the foliage. . . . Now could be beheld that change from the handsome to the curious which the features of a wood undergo at the ingress of the winter months. Angles were taking the place of curves, and reticulations of surfaces—a change constituting a sudden lapse from the ornate to the primitive, and comparable to a retrogressive step from the art of an advanced school of painting to that of the pacific islander.[8]

This is Hardy at his clumsiest, but the passage is far from being uncharacteristic. Phrases like "at the ingress of the winter months" and "comparable to a retrogressive step" have all the marks of Victorian journalese; and the man who could write of the plantations and copses "in which a more tardy leave-taking than on windy summits was the rule with the foliage" seems to be suffering from a sort of literary arthritis. (That Hardy should not have noticed and suppressed the concealed pun of "leave-taking" and "leaf-taking" is a startling indication of his frequent insensitiveness to words.) On the whole, however, Victorian prose suffered less in an industrial age than most of the other arts; it had a practical function to perform, and it stayed reasonably close to daily life. It worked, it was usually efficient, it kept on going. If it gives little positive pleasure, it rarely gives actual pain—unlike the painting and sculpture of the period, which were for the most part produced in a cultural vacuum.

II

It is only too easy to oversimplify the nineteenth century. Was it, for instance, as Matthew Arnold kept telling it, an age in which Englishmen rejoiced in doing what they liked, an age of aggressive individualism and nonconformity? The evidence is conflicting. The nineteenth century, it is true, opened in a period of revolution; and in England the literary movement of the first two or three decades encouraged the assertion of individuality and the cult of personality. While critics like Jeffrey kept insisting that literature must be based on "general and ordinary nature," and criticized writers like Goethe and Wordsworth as unnatural, fantastic, improbable, affected, and so on, the writers themselves continued to show a considerable interest in the odd, the unfamiliar, the individual, and even the unique. It is not surprising that the cult of the individual should have spread to prose style, and the emphasis have shifted from communication to self-expression. Charles Lamb, for one, evolved a highly personal idiom, derived from his fondness for the literature of the seventeenth century and from his own gentle, dreaming personality. If a writer is going to exploit his personality, he had better make sure that it is an attractive one. What, to most readers, is pleasing in Lamb, may be thoroughly displeasing in Leigh Hunt, whose personality is of poorer quality, and whose facetiousness and self-conscious airs and graces are at times unspeakably banal. In the following passage he is writing "On the Graces and Anxieties of Pig-Driving":

The title is a little startling; but "style and sentiment," as a lady said, "can do anything." Remember, then, gentle reader, that talents are not to be despised in the humblest walks of life; we will add, nor in the muddiest. The other day we happened to be among a set of spectators who could not help stopping to admire the patience and address with which a pig-driver huddled and cherished onward his drove of unaccommodating *élèves*, down a street in the suburbs. He was a born genius for a manœuvre. Had he originated in a higher sphere he would have been a general, or a stage-manager, or, at least, the head of a set of monks. Conflicting interests were his forte; pig-headed wills and proceedings hopeless. To see the *hand* with which he did it! How hovering, yet firm; how encouraging, yet compelling; how indicative of the space on each side of him, and yet of the line before him; how general, how particular, how perfect! No barber's could quiver about a head with more lightness of apprehension; no cook's pat up and proportion the side of a pasty with a more final eye. The whales, quoth old Chapman, speaking of Neptune,

The whales exulted under him, and knew their mighty king.

The pigs did not exult, but they knew their king. Unwilling was their subjection, but "more in sorrow than in anger." They were too far gone for rage. Their case was hopeless. They did not see why they should proceed; but they felt themselves bound to do so; forced, conglomerated, crowded onwards, irrestistibly compelled by fate and Jenkins. . . .[9]

And so it goes on, with the pigs "eschewing the tip-end of the whip of office," and casting "shrewd backward glances," until we feel inclined to cry, "Pox! leave thy damnable faces, and begin!" The essayist, being more apt than most writers to have nothing very much to say, is always in danger of substituting stylistic mannerism for matter. Too often he is driven back on narcissistic reverie, shyly doting on his own whimsical personality. There is something of this even in Addison; but at least the eighteenth-century essayist usually expressed himself through a *persona*, a Mr. Spectator or an Isaac Bickerstaff; whereas Leigh Hunt is unashamedly, delightedly, and ostentatiously himself.*

The prose of Hazlitt, on the other hand, is quite free from this narcissistic element, because however personal Hazlitt's style may be, and however impressionistic his criticism, he is always trying to realize and report on something outside himself. "There are some people who cannot taste olives," he will tell us, "and I cannot much relish Ben Jonson."[10] But after clearing the air with this petulant outburst, he proceeds to deal fairly enough with Jonson—with the impression that Jonson's plays have made upon him. Hazlitt's prose—and much of it, of course, is lecture talk—is always lively and colloquial. But the best prose written during the Romantic period is perhaps to be found in the letters of Keats, where we can constantly observe the genesis and growth of ideas in his mind, and where the writing responds with wonderful fidelity to the form and pressure of his thought.

On the whole, the exploiters of personality belong to the earlier rather than to the later half of the nineteenth century. But the tendency to be oneself at all costs is seen at its most violent and intractable in the prose of Thomas Carlyle. The Victorians might not have liked all their authors to gesticulate in print and explode about their ears after the fashion of Carlyle, but his high reputation in later life seems to show that his cultivated violence and eccentricity made a deep impression on them. Carlyle was in some ways a reincarnation of the seventeenth-century Puritan, burning with zeal and confidence in his own rightness, and exerting the authority of a field-preacher over

*According to Hunt (*Autobiography*, ed. J. E. Morpurgo [1949], p. 416) this essay was "hailed as one of my best pieces of writing." Carlyle, writing to Hunt, 8 April, 1834, called it "a most tickling thing" and praised its "subquizzical sweet-acid geniality of mockery."

men and women who mistook positive assertion for truth. He despised the eighteenth century and all that it stood for: its politeness and restraint were to him insincerity; its rationalism, spiritual timidity; its scepticism and dislike of enthusiasm, the measure of its own lack of inspiration. No writer of the period believed more firmly than Carlyle that all art, and indeed all worthy human achievement, sprang from the vision, the intuition, the inner light of the inspired individual. The earlier Romantics had their roots in the eighteenth century and retained some of its intellectual discipline; but Carlyle, the Scottish peasant's son, had the dedicated conviction of the seventeenth-century Covenanters—that stubborn confidence in a personal revelation that made Cromwell exclaim to the General Assembly of the Kirk of Scotland in 1650: "I beseech you, in the bowels of Christ, think it possible you may be mistaken." I cannot therefore question Carlyle's sincerity, any more than I would question that of D. H. Lawrence: as they felt, so they both believed. But I am not prepared to accept with equal confidence the sincerity of Carlyle's prose style. In that, there was unquestionably something of the charlatan. I choose a passage from *Past and Present* in which, characteristically, he is haranguing the reader:

And again, hast thou valued Patience, Courage, Perseverance, Openness to light; readiness to own thyself mistaken, to do better next time? All these, all virtues, in wrestling with the dim brute Powers of Fact, in ordering of thy fellows in such wrestle, there and elsewhere not at all, thou wilt continually learn. Set down a brave Sir Christopher in the middle of black ruined Stone-heaps, of foolish unarchitectural Bishops, redtape Officials, idle Nell-Gwyn Defenders of the Faith; and see whether he will ever raise a Paul's Cathedral out of all that, yea or no! Rough, rude, contradictory are all things and persons, from the mutinous masons and Irish hodmen, up to the idle Nell-Gwyn Defenders, to blustering redtape Officials, foolish unarchitectural Bishops. All these things and persons are there not for Christopher's sake and his Cathedral's; they are there for their own sake mainly! Christopher will have to conquer and constrain all these,— if he is able. All these are against him. Equitable Nature herself, who carries her mathematics and architectonics not on the face of her, but deep in the hidden heart of her,—Nature herself is but partially for him; will be wholly against him, if he constrain her not! His very money, where is it to come from? The pious munificence of England lies far-scattered, distant, unable to speak, and say, "I am here"—must be spoken to before it can speak. Pious munificence, and all help, is so silent, invisible like the gods; impediment, contradictions manifold are so loud and near! O brave Sir Christopher, trust thou in those notwithstanding, and front all these; understand all these; by valiant patience, noble effort, insight, by man's strength, vanquish and compel all these,—and, on the whole, strike down victoriously the last topstone of that Paul's Edifice; thy monument for certain centuries, the stamp "Great Man" impressed very legibly on Portland-stone there![11]

It would be difficult to say what was Carlyle's natural voice when he was putting his thoughts on paper, but I would look for it in his familiar letters and *Reminiscences* rather than in *Sartor Resartus* or *Past and Present* or *The French Revolution*. I imagine that we come as near to the natural man as we are ever likely to get with Carlyle when we read the letter he wrote to his brother on 23 March, 1835. He had recently suffered a grievous loss: the manuscript of the first volume of his *French Revolution*, on which he had been at work for months, had been destroyed by a careless housemaid of John Stuart Mill's. When Carlyle sat down to write to his brother three weeks later, he had recovered from the first shock, and already he was able to contemplate the whole disastrous episode at a distance, and to tell the story with a certain amount of detachment. But the feeling was still there, and the affair was still too serious and too immediately personal to allow much room for histrionics and literary flourishes; and besides, Carlyle was not writing for the Victorian public, but to his brother, a sensible Scot who would not have thanked him if he had been addressed in the style of *Heroes and Hero-Worship*.

My Dear Brother,

Your Letter came in this morning (after sixteen days from Rome); and, tomorrow being post-day, I have shoved my writing-table into the corner, and sit (with my back to the fire and Jane, who is busy sewing at my old jupe of a Dressing-gown) forthwith making answer. It was somewhat longed-for; yet I felt, in other respects, that it was better you had not written sooner; for I had a thing to dilate upon, of a most ravelled character, that was better to be knit up a little first. You shall hear. But do not be alarmed; for it is "neither death nor men's lives": we are all well, and I heard out of Annandale within these three weeks, nay, Jane's Newspaper came with the customary "two strokes" only five days ago. I meant to write to our Mother last night; but shall now do it tomorrow.

Mill had borrowed that first Volume of my poor *French Revolution* (pieces of it more than once) that he might have it all before him, and write down some observations on it, which perhaps I might print as Notes. I was busy meanwhile with Volume Second; toiling along like a *Nigger*, but with the heart of a free Roman: indeed, I know not how it was, I had not felt so clear and independent, sure of myself and of my task for many long years. Well, one night about three weeks ago, we sat at tea, and Mill's short rap was heard at the door: Jane rose to welcome him; but he stood there unresponsive, pale, the very picture of despair; said, half-articulately gasping, that she must go down and speak to Mrs. Taylor. . . . After some considerable additional gasping, I learned from Mill this fact: that my poor Manuscript, all except some four tattered leaves, was *annihilated!* He had left it out (too carelessly); it had been taken for waste paper: and so five months of as tough labour as I could remember of, were as good as vanished, gone like a whiff of smoke.—There never in my life had come upon me any other *accident* of much moment; but this I could not but feel to be a sore one. The thing was *lost*, and perhaps worse; for I had not only forgotten all the structure of it, but the spirit it was written with was past; only the general impression seemed to remain, and the recollection that I was on the whole well satisfied with that, and could now hardly hope to equal it. Mill whom I had to comfort and speak peace to remained injudiciously enough till almost midnight, and my poor Dame and I had to sit talking of indifferent matters; and could not till then get our lament freely uttered. *She* was very good to me, and the thing did not beat us. I felt in general that I was as a little Schoolboy, who had laboriously written out his *Copy* as he could, and was showing it not without satisfaction to the Master: but lo! the Master had suddenly torn it, saying: "No, boy, thou must go and write it *better*." . . .[12]

There is still a considerable element of the exclamatory and the emphatic about Carlyle's narrative here: the loss of the manuscript, after all, was the sort of dramatic event that appealed to his histrionic sense. But compared with the passage from *Past and Present,* this letter is simple and natural, and towards the end undeniably moving. For addressing his public, however, Carlyle the author had evolved an artificial, tortured, falsetto, and exclamatory style that we should normally associate with a literary mountebank. We must not allow the apparent spontaneity to deceive us: the spontaneity is deliberate, a highly mannered thing, even if in time it must have become a sort of second nature from repeated use. Much of Carlyle's prose (and the passage from *Past and Present* is a fair example) has all the marks of the fanatical preacher: conscious emphasis, repetition for rhetorical effect, apostrophe, exclamation and interrogation, archaism, a ruthless manhandling of English idiom, every kind of shock and surprise. For a page or two we may be compelled to listen; but Carlyle has cried "Wolf! wolf!" so often and so loudly that sooner or later we cease to pay attention. How far his adoption of this strange and rhetorical utterance was due to the fact that he was of Scottish peasant stock, and could not trust himself to write plain idiomatic English, it would be hard to say; but that, together with the fact that he was a sort of displaced person in London, may have had something to do with it.

Carlyle is an extreme case of nineteenth-century individualism, of doing what one likes. But there were others who, in one form or another, carried their writing to a pitch of eccentricity that would have seemed excessive to the eighteenth-century reader, and that provoked even some Victorians to protest. One of those writers was George Meredith. Yet though Meredith is sometimes wilfully eccentric, his odd and surprising metaphors are often highly functional, revealing a whole situation in a flash. In *The Egoist,* for example, he is remarkably successful in making us realize and understand the changing attitude of Clara Middleton to Sir Willoughby Patterne, the man to whom she has somehow or other allowed herself to become engaged, and whom she now sees, more and more clearly every day, as a pompous and quite appalling egoist. What would marriage to such a man be like?

To be fixed at the mouth of a mine, and to have to descend it daily, and not to discover great opulence below; on the contrary to be

chilled in subterranean sunlessness, without any substantial quality
that she could grasp, only the mystery of inefficient tallow-light in
those caverns of the complacent talking man: this appeared to her
too extreme a probation for two or three weeks. How of a lifetime
of it![13]

Or again:

She conceived the state of marriage with him as that of a woman
tied not to a man of heart, but to an obelisk lettered all over with
hieroglyphics, and everlastingly hearing him expound them, relish-
ingly renewing his lectures on them.[14]

Sir Willoughby comes before us in a series of slightly ludicrous
metaphors—"chewing the cud in the happy pastures of un-
awakenedness," believing "the whole bulk of his personality to
be sustained" upon "the full river of [Clara's] love." Or we meet
him in the presence of the patient and acquiescent Laetitia Dale:
"The presence of Miss Dale illuminated him as the burning
taper lights up consecrated plate."[15] Without such original
metaphor, precise but also charged with suggestion, Meredith's
novels would lose much of their power to penetrate the reader's
defences. With him the metaphor is more than a figurative way
of expressing plain facts and abstract ideas; it frequently enables
us, as no other method would, to realize the innermost thoughts
and feelings of his characters. Isolated from their context—and,
still more, lifted for the purposes of criticism like fish from the
water—Meredith's metaphors may seem too elaborate and artificial; but when we come upon them in their own Meredithian
element they seem entirely natural. Despite the strain of wil-
fulness and conscious mannerism in much of Meredith's writing,
it must be admitted that his eccentricity is often forced upon him
because he is probing into obscure corners of human personality
that had not hitherto been explored, and recording what he has
found in words that startle us into sudden realization. Such
subtlety was not very common in the Victorian period; we have
become much more accustomed to it in the present century in
the novels of Henry James, Virginia Woolf, E. M. Forster, and
many others.

III

The closing decades of the nineteenth century saw some rather unhappy attempts to write in a finer and more precious style than that of the honest utilitarian prose which had been good enough for the average writer during the greater part of the Victorian age. Now, in the 1880's Walter Pater took off on some sustained flights of heightened and almost poetic prose, and he was followed by Oscar Wilde and other writers of the 1890's. Ruskin and William Morris had already written in a fashion that hovered uneasily between prose and poetry, and that left their readers in a state of willing but rather blurred exaltation. This consciously fine writing asked for, and often got, a correspondingly precious print and binding, and led to that abomination, "the book beautiful." Prose was straying again from its proper function, and becoming an end product rather than a means. I have no sympathy with this sort of writing, and am not therefore likely to do justice to it. But it can be (to use one of Mr. Evelyn Waugh's expressions) quite "shaming." I cite as an example a passage from John Addington Symonds, one of the most applauded authors of this poetic prose:

The full moon was partly hidden by heavy clouds, but the northern sky held delicate green and pale-blue light, and the moon poured oblique rays upon the river and the woods. Then the clouds sailed slowly away, and their edges were tinct with pearl and opal. Spaces of crystalline azure, seas of glass, swam between them, full-filled with moonlight and trembling with scattered stars—stars scarcely seen in the pellucid radiance—stars palpitating, throbbing out breathless melodies. At length the moon emerged, naked and round, glorious, midway above the bridge, suspended in luminous twilight. The cliff shone like marble in her plenilunar splendour. But again the clouds gathered. A vulture's head shot forward and swallowed the moon's silver sphere. Again she triumphed, and this time the clouds dispersed in gauze and filmy veils of faintest shell-like hues. Finally Queen Luna reigned in undisputed majesty. . . .[16]

This ornate passage is characteristically loaded with adjectives and with literary and semi-obsolete expressions like "tinct," "full-filled," and "shell-like hues," and it is drenched with colours that in combination leave only a confused impression on the mind. The words, one suspects, are used less for their sense than for their sound: "crystalline azure," "pellucid radiance," "plenilunar splendour." As Symonds's eloquence goes more and more to his head, the moon passes from being an inanimate satellite to being "she," and finally suffers a total eclipse of respectability in the banal periphrasis of "Queen Luna." The stars which are "scarcely seen in the pellucid radiance" nevertheless palpitate and throb and tremble. The very sentence rhythms are misleading, and fail to suggest what is going on. The author has set out to describe the night sky, with the clouds sailing slowly across the face of the moon, and then opening again to leave the sky bare. But this gradual change cannot be conveyed to us in the abrupt style of Macaulay describing a battle:

The cliff shone like marble in her plenilunar splendour. But again the clouds gathered. A vulture's head shot forward and swallowed the moon's silver sphere. Again she triumphed. . . .

One would be willing to pass over such writers as John Addington Symonds in silence if the sort of florid writing in which he habitually indulged was not continually being held up as fine prose, and inserted in the anthologies.* It is not prose, but poetry gone bad.

IV

When we reach the twentieth century, even the broad generalizations in which I have been dealing become more and more difficult to make. But I will venture upon two. Modern prose has become, like modern manners and modern dress, a good deal less formal than it usually was in the nineteenth century; and it has come closer and closer to reproducing the mental processes of the writer, or (if he is a novelist) of his characters. With the loosening of the old regular metres and the general abandonment of stanza forms in modern poetry, it is hardly

*Cf. the review in The Spectator, quoted at the back of the third edition, 1918: "Descriptions of scenery, always touched with supreme skill. . . ."

surprising that a similar urge for freedom of movement has been felt in prose. At present prose style is probably more colloquial than it has ever been before, or, at any rate, since the days of Defoe. It is in keeping with this modern tendency that more and more writers, such as Miss Ivy Compton Burnett and Mr. Henry Green, give us novels which are almost entirely in dialogue. When the dialogue is less frequent, as in the novels of Virginia Woolf, we may still be getting the unspoken thoughts of the characters expressed in a kind of silent conversation or monologue.

Conversation, it is true, will vary greatly with the occasion, and with the education of the speaker or his hearers. It may range from the elaborate to the casual and off-hand, and from the involved and even artificial structure to the loose and ungrammatical. For an example of modern prose based on a highly deliberate and involved conversation, we cannot do better than turn to Henry James. In selecting a passage from *A Small Boy and Others*, I am less concerned to show James at his best than to indicate his manner, or at least his later manner, of writing. *A Small Boy and Others* is a sort of prolonged reverie in which James looks back at his childhood. In this passage he is describing a dance to which he had been taken at a very early age:

It took place in the house of our cousins Robert and Kitty Emmet the elder—for we were to have two cousin Kittys of that ilk and yet another consanguineous Robert at least; the latter name being naturally, amongst them all, of a pious, indeed of a glorious, tradition, and three of my father's nieces marrying three Emmet brothers, the first of these the Robert aforesaid. Catherine James, daughter of my uncle Augustus, his then quite recent, and, as I remember her, animated and attractive bride, whose fair hair framed her pointed smile in full and far-drooping "front" curls, I easily invoke as my first apprehended image of the free and happy young woman of fashion, a sign of the wondrous fact that ladies might live for pleasure, pleasure always, pleasure alone. She was distinguished for nothing whatever so much as for an insatiable love of the dance; that passion in which I think of the "good," the best, New York society of the time as having capered and champagned itself away. Her younger sister Gertrude, afterwards married to James—or more inveterately Jim—Pendleton, of Virginia, followed close upon her heels, literally speaking, and though emulating her in other respects too, was to last, through many troubles, much longer (looking extraordinarily the while like the younger portraits of Queen Victoria) and to have much hospitality, showing it, and showing everything, in a singularly natural way, for a considerable collection of young hobbledehoy kinsmen.[17]

Like most of James's later writing, this passage was dictated to a secretary, and then revised; it not only reads like a man talking, it actually *is* a record of the speaking voice. We are conscious of a mind thinking, with all the hesitations and pauses, the afterthoughts, the effort to obtain a more precise definition or a more inclusive statement. But it would be naïve to suppose that James was just rambling along disconnectedly; he only *wishes* to give us the impression that his mind is journeying freely through the past. On the whole, however, the order in which his ideas are set down probably represents fairly closely the way in which they presented themselves to his mind; and even when the order appears to be artificial, it was probably natural to James. In the second sentence, for instance, he does not begin by telling us, "I can easily remember Catherine James"; he begins with what is presumably uppermost in his mind at the moment, the girl herself, whose "full and far-drooping 'front' curls" and whose "pointed smile" are still etched in his memory, and only then faces up to the demands of syntax, and proceeds with the words, "I easily invoke." No doubt this is a special kind of talk, far from being unpremeditated, and considerably corrected and amplified before publication; but it is a fair approximation to James's conversation, and it does bring us close to the mind at work.*

*It is only fair to quote James's reply to a lady who attributed his later style to his habit of dictation:

"And dictating, please, has moreover nothing to do with it. The value of that process for me is in its help to do over and over, for which it is extremely adapted, and which is the only way I can do at all. It soon enough, accordingly, becomes, *intellectually* absolutely identical with the act of writing—or has become so, after five years now, with me; so that the difference is only material and illusory—only the difference, that is, that I walk up and down: which is so much to the good."

(*The Letters of Henry James*, ed. Percy Lubbock [1920], I, Letter to Mrs. Cadwalader Jones, 23 October, 1902.)

Perhaps the most serious objection to this kind of composition is that James has so many parentheses and afterthoughts that the syntactical pattern is apt to be lost in the qualifying phrases and clauses, and we sometimes lose (or James himself has already lost) the rhythm of the sentence. No one, I imagine, would be likely to claim that the prose of Henry James is suited for all, or even for many, purposes. In so far as it is not purely personal to him, it may perhaps, with its striving after precision and inclusiveness, be called academic prose. Something of the same kind, though with less of the agonized searching for the irreplaceably right word, may be found in the writings of George Saintsbury: a sort of good lecture talk, easy with the rather ponderous ease of professors when they are consciously trying to appear relaxed. A recent letter in the *Times Literary Supplement* will serve to show that the influence of the Master is by no means extinct. A well-known critic is replying to a reviewer:

SIR,—Middleton Murry adduced as illustrating Lawrence's "rooted sadistic hatred" and his "adoption of a primitive mindlessness" (your reviewer's phrases—I refer to the review of Murry's *Love, Freedom and Society* in your issue for March 29) the passage about the West African figure in chapter XIX of *Women in Love*. I pointed out that Murry here (and very characteristically), through ignoring the nature of that closely organized novel as a work of art, was guilty of a demonstrable and complete misrepresentation of Lawrence—a reversal of the truth. I did this in the course of examining the "construction" (organization, I myself should prefer to call it) of *Women in Love*, for in examining the "construction" I was—how could it be otherwise?—examining the complexity of thought, attitude, and valuation (the significance) that Lawrence's art was devoted to conveying. Your reviewer says that "it is to the enjoyment of the style and construction of particular works that Dr. Leavis calls us," and he seems to agree with Murry at any rate to the extent of allowing that there may be some better and surer way of arriving at Lawrence's essential communication. ("Enjoyment" is not the word that comes first—I, it's agreed, am still "austere"—to me, but if we "enjoy" *Lear* and *Anna Karenina* the word will do for *Women in Love*.) Murry himself, of course, could claim—he made a point of claiming—to have known Lawrence personally (Lawrence had another view of the matter). Perhaps we are to take this as constituting a conceivable

advantage of Murry's as an authority on Lawrence's *"Existenz"* (give
me inverted commas as well as italics, please)—a word which, when
linked with "message," suggests that this is some profound kind of
significance beyond the purview of a mere "enjoyer" of style and
construction. This possibility, however, only confirms my strong feeling that *"Existenz"* is a term I would rather take no risk of being
supposed to be associating myself with. . . .[18]

Such prose as that, one would guess, could only be written by a
man who was used to holding the floor and talking without fear
of interruption; and perhaps the colloquial deliberateness and
the parenthetic asides and hesitations of so much academic prose
are not altogether to be dissociated from the tutorial and the
seminar, where the omniscient don is accustomed to giving laws
to his little senate of undergraduates.

To find a prose style sufficiently flexible for the modern tem-
per, and yet not too personal to serve as an example to the modern
writer, I turn to D. H. Lawrence. The passage I quote is from
a letter to Lady Ottoline Morrell, written in the first year of the
First World War. The familiar letter is, of course, in a special
category; and yet this letter is a fair example of that intense and
sensitive, yet natural and colloquial, prose that Lawrence nearly
always wrote. He is writing on May 14, 1915, from the rural
depths of Sussex:

We were in London for four days: beautiful weather, but I don't
like London. My eyes can see nothing human that is good, nowadays; at any rate, nothing public. London seems to me like some
hoary massive underworld, a hoary ponderous inferno. The traffic
flows through the rigid grey streets like the rivers of hell through
their banks of dry, rocky ash. The fashions and the women's clothes
are very ugly.

Coming back here, I find the country very beautiful. The apple
trees are leaning forwards, all white with blossom, towards the green
grass. I watch, in the morning when I wake up, a thrush on the wall
outside the window—not a thrush, a blackbird—and he sings, opening his beak. It is a strange thing to watch his singing, opening his
beak and giving out his calls and warblings, and then remaining
silent. He looks so remote, so buried in primeval silence, standing
there on the wall, and bethinking himself, then opening his beak to

make the strange, strong sounds. He seems as if his singing were a sort of talking to himself, or of thinking aloud his strongest thoughts. I wish I was a blackbird, like him. I hate men. . . .

The bluebells are all out in the wood, under the new vivid leaves. But they are rather dashed by yesterday's rain. It would be nice if the Lord sent another flood and drowned the world. Probably I should want to be Noah. I am not sure.

I've got again into one of those horrible sleeps from which I can't wake. I can't brush it aside to wake up. You know those horrible sleeps when one is struggling to wake up, and can't. I was like it all autumn—now I am again like it. Everything has a touch of delirium, the blackbird on the wall is a delirium, even the apple-blossom. And when I see a snake winding rapidly in the marshy places, I think I am mad.

It is not a question of me, it is the world of men. The world of men is dreaming, it has gone mad in its sleep, and a snake is strangling it, but it can't wake up. . . .[19]

This is the prose of a poet, but it is not poetic prose. Lawrence's sentences are short; his thoughts are set down (as so often were those of Keats in his letters) more or less as they occur to his mind. There is no undue deliberation, almost no trace of anything that could be called "literary"; and yet this is the prose of a man who is concentrating intensely on what he is saying, who is entirely sincere, and who is setting down an experience sharply focused. There is some repetition, but it is the repetition of a man puzzling over his experience, and seeking for a clearer definition of it—trying to express a whole situation and a state of mind. The style of the passage is a sort of controlled colloquialism; it is the voice of the twentieth century, unencumbered by dead or moribund idioms and phrases, or by stylistic echoes of the past. But in the prose of Lawrence we find, too, what is not necessarily characteristic of the twentieth century: the same single-minded devotion to the idea or experience to be expressed as we find in the great Puritan writers, the same abhorrence of airs and graces and decoration of any kind. Such qualities are always impressive, wherever we find them; they are never likely to be common.

In conclusion, I will set beside Lawrence a writer of a very different kind, one of his own contemporaries, to see whether we cannot find a common element that we can call modern. In Virginia Woolf we have a writer who belonged, much more than Lawrence, to the humane tradition of English letters. Virginia Woolf had literature in her blood; she grew up in a literary household, and she was in the milieu of polite letters all her life. We must therefore be prepared to find in her writing less of the naked simplicity of Lawrence, and more of the overtones of culture, and the nice discrimination of the sophisticated. Yet in her untiring search for immediacy of experience, in her unfailing effort to seize upon and express the moment as it passes, she is as modern as Lawrence or Joyce. The passage I have chosen— from an essay on Sidney's *Arcadia*—shows her at work, not on life, but on literature; but it is marked by the same sensitive recording of impressions as we find in her novels. She pays a tribute to the freshness and loveliness of Sidney's imaginary world, his pleasure in words, and the undulating rhythm of his sentences. First impressions are altogether delightful; and then, gradually, the delight gives place to a gentle ennui:

And as the story winds on its way, or rather as the succession of stories fall on each other like soft snowflakes, one obliterating the other, we are much tempted to follow their example. Sleep weighs down our eyes. Half dreaming, half yawning, we prepare to seek the elder brother of death. What, then, has become of that first intoxicating sense of freedom? We who wished to escape have been caught and enmeshed. Yet how easy it seemed in the beginning to tell a story to amuse a sister—how inspiriting to escape from here and now and wander wildly in a world of lutes and roses! But alas! softness has weighed down our steps; brambles have caught at our clothing. We have come to long for some plain statement, and the decoration of the style, at first so enchanting, has dulled and decayed. It is not difficult to find the reason. High spirited, flown with words, Sidney seized his pen too carelessly. He had no notion when he set out where he was going. Telling stories, he thought, was enough— one could follow another interminably. But where there is no end in view there is no sense of direction to draw us on. . . . So by degrees the book floats away into the thin air of limbo. It becomes one of those half-forgotten and deserted places where the grasses grow over fallen statues and the rain drips and the marble steps are green with moss and vast weeds flourish in the flower-beds. And yet it is a beautiful garden to wander in now and then; one stumbles over lovely broken faces, and here and there a flower blooms and the nightingale sings in the lilac tree.[20]

I am not now concerned with the value of this passage as literary criticism, though I do not share the modern contempt for impressionistic criticism when it is as good as this. But there can surely be no doubt about the quality of the writing. Virginia Woolf's sentences evoke with remarkable delicacy the timeless atmosphere of Sidney's rambling story, partly by her use of imagery, and partly by the gentle falling rhythms that faintly echo Sidney's own haunting cadences. In some ways the writing is very different from that of Lawrence—much richer in imagery, more deliberate, more studied, and more dependent on literary allusions; but the common element is there, and I have already suggested what it is. What Lawrence and Virginia Woolf have in common is an essential simplicity and directness of sentence structure; they have returned, after the greater formality and occasional pomposity of nineteenth-century prose, to something much closer to the colloquial. It must be apparent by now that this is the sort of prose I have been holding up for admiration. I can only hope that in showing my own preference I have not been unjust to the more elaborate and ornate splendours of Sir Thomas Browne and Jeremy Taylor in the seventeenth century, or John Ruskin and Walter Pater in the nineteenth.

In what I have had to say about English prose I have dealt for the most part only with the common elements in the writing of different periods. The meshes of my net have been so wide that it may be thought that everything that distinguishes the individual writer from his contemporaries has slipped through. I have said little about those qualities which are usually taken to be most personal to an author—humour, good humour, irony, gravity, intellectual lucidity, restraint and under-statement, fastidiousness, robustness, grandeur and grandiosity, humility, affectation, and many more. To do so would have meant analysing in detail the work of many different writers. But I hope I can plead justification for what I have done, or tried to do. If I have dealt mainly with those features of prose style which are common to the most characteristic writers of each period, my justification must be that it is only after those common elements have been clearly recognized that the evaluation of individuals can usefully begin.

NOTES

NOTES

CHAPTER I

1. W. P. Ker, in *English Prose Selections*, ed. Henry Craik (1893), I.10.
2. *Boswell's Life of Johnson*, ed. G. B. Hill and L. F. Powell (1934), I.192.
3. *The Lyfe of Sir Thomas Moore, Knighte*, ed. Elsie Hitchcock (1935), Early English Text Society, CXCVII.30–32.
4. *The Faerie Queene*, V.ii.39–43.
5. Heminge and Condell, "To the great Variety of Readers," in the First Folio.
6. H. B. Chaytor, *From Script to Print* (1945), p. 10.
7. Morris W. Croll, "Attic Prose in the Seventeenth Century," *Studies in Philology*, XVIII (1921).90–92.
8. "A Schort Reule of Lif," *Select English Works of John Wyclif*, ed. Thomas Arnold (1869–71), III.207.
9. *The Works of Sir Thomas Malory*, ed. Eugène Vinaver (1947), III.1229–30.
10. Herbert Spencer, *The Principles of Sociology* (1877), I.536.
11. *Troilus and Criseyde*, V.1793–98.
12. W. P. Ker, in *English Prose Selections*, I.12.
13. Ralph Lever, *The Arte of Reason* (1573); quoted by R. F. Jones, *The Triumph of the English Language* (1953), p. 69.
14. Richard Mulcaster, *The First Part of the Elementarie*, ed. E. T. Campagnac (1925), pp. 172–73; quoted by R. F. Jones, *The Triumph of the English Language*, pp. 69–70.
15. Roger Ascham, *Toxophilus*, ed. Edward Arber (1868), p. 18.
16. *Elizabethan Critical Essays*, ed. G. Gregory Smith (1904), I.357.
17. Shakespeare, *Troilus and Cressida*, I.iii.94ff.
18. R. F. Jones, *The Triumph of the English Language*, p. 30.

19. John Brinsley, *Ludus Literarius, or the Grammar Schoole*, ed. E. T. Campagnac (1917), p. 219.
20. *Ibid.*, pp. 20–21.
21. John Locke, *Some Thoughts Concerning Education*, § 189; ed. R. H. Quick (1884), p. 165.
22. H. S. Bennett, *Chaucer and the Fifteenth Century*, "Oxford History of English Literature" (1947), p. 180.
23. F. P. Wilson, *Elizabethan and Jacobean* (1945), pp. 50–51.
24. Samuel Johnson, Preface to Shakespeare; *Shakespeare Criticism: A Selection*, ed. D. Nichol Smith (1916), p. 101.
25. S. T. Coleridge, *The Table Talk and Omniana* . . . , ed. T. Ashe (1888), p. 238.
26. Sir Thomas Browne, *Works*, ed. Geoffrey Keynes (1928–31), VI.230.

CHAPTER II

1. Francis Bacon, *The Advancement of Learning*, Bk. I, ch.iv, § 2.
2. Translated by Izora Scott, *Controversies over the Imitation of Cicero*, pt. ii, p. 24; quoted by George Williamson, *The Senecan Amble* (London, 1951), pp. 12–13.
3. See, for example, *The Vulgaria of John Stanbridge and the Vulgaria of Robert Whittinton*, ed. Beatrice White (1933), EETS, Original Series, No. 187.
4. Roger Ascham, *The Scholemaster* (1570), ed. Edward Arber (1932), p. 155.
5. *Ibid.*, pp. 111–12.
6. John Lyly, *Endymion*, III.iv; *The Complete Works of John Lyly*, ed. R. Warwick Bond (1902), III.50.
7. *The Complete Works of Sir Philip Sidney*, ed. A. Feuillerat (1922), I.13.
8. Ben Jonson, *Timber, or Discoveries*; in *Critical Essays of the Seventeenth Century*, ed. J. E. Spingarn (1908), I.19.
9. *Longinus on the Sublime*, trans. A. O. Prickard (1906), pp. 46–47 (§ xxii).
10. Ben Jonson, *Timber, or Discoveries*; *ed. cit.*, I.26.
11. Bacon, *Advancement of Learning*, Bk. II, ch. xvii, § 4.

12. *Ibid.*, Bk. II, ch. xvii, § 6.
13. *Ibid.*, Bk. I, ch. v, § 9.
14. *Essays of John Dryden*, ed. W. P. Ker (1900), I.155.
15. William Wordsworth, "Essay, Supplementary to the Preface"; *Wordsworth's Literary Criticism*, ed. Nowell C. Smith (1905), p. 198.
16. Thomas Love Peacock, *Headlong Hall*, ed. George Saintsbury (1927), pp. 45–46 (ch. iv).
17. Sir Philip Sidney, *An Apology for Poetry*; in *Elizabethan Critical Essays*, ed. G. Gregory Smith (1904), I.187.
18. Bacon, *The Advancement of Learning*, Bk. II, ch. xvii, § 4.
19. *Ibid.*, Bk. I, ch. viii, § 1.
20. *Coleridge's Miscellaneous Criticism*, ed. T. M. Raysor (1936), pp. 226–27.
21. *The Works of That Learned and Judicious Divine, Mr. Richard Hooker . . .* , ed. Rev. John Keble (1874), I.198.
22. *The Theological Works of Isaac Barrow, D.D.*, ed. Alexander Napier (1859), II.3–4.
23. S. T. Coleridge, *Biographia Literaria*, ed. W. Shawcross (1907), II.44 (ch. xviii).
24. Thomas Fuller, *The Church History of Britain*, ed. J. S. Brewer (1845), I.183.
25. *The Works of Thomas Nashe*, ed. R. B. McKerrow (1904–10), III.197–99 (*Nashe's Lenten Stuffe*).
26. Translated by Basil Anderton, *Sketches from a Library Window* (1923), pp. 29–30; quoted by George Williamson, *The Senecan Amble*, p. III.
27. F. P. Wilson, *Elizabethan and Jacobean* (1945), pp. 31–32.
28. *The Works of Joseph Hall . . .* (1625), p. 193 (*Characters of Vertues & Vices*, "Of the Covetous").
29. Robert Burton, *The Anatomy of Melancholy*, Bohn's Standard Library (1893), pp. 30–31.
30. David Lloyd, *The States-men and Favourites of England Since the Reformation . . .* (1665), pp. 450–51.
31. Francis Bacon, *De Augmentis Scientiarum*, trans. Gilbert Wats (1640), p. 29.
32. Bacon, *The Advancement of Learning*, Bk. II, ch. xvii, § 4. Cf. p. 42.
33. Thomas Sprat, *A History of the Royal Society* (1667), Pt. II, § xx.

CHAPTER III

1. Walter Pater, *The Renaissance* (1915 ed.), p. xi (Preface).
2. *Mercurius Aulicus*, 1 Jan. 1643.
3. Reproduced in facsimile in *Tracts on Liberty in the Puritan Revolution*, ed. William Haller (1934), III.[353].
4. Richard Baxter, *Gildas Salvianus* (1656); *The Practical Works of Richard Baxter* (1707), IV.358; quoted by Harold Fisch, "The Puritans and the Reform of Prose Style," *ELH*, XIX (1952), 229ff.
5. Thomas Hobbes, *Leviathan*, ed. Michael Oakeshott (1947), pp. 21–22 (Pt. I, ch. iv).
6. *Essays of John Dryden*, ed. W. P. Ker (1900), I.259.
7. *The Dramatic Works of John Dryden* (1717): Dedication by William Congreve. See also D. Nichol Smith, *John Dryden* (1950), pp. 88–90.
8. Thomas Sprat, *A History of the Royal Society* (1667), Pt. II, § xx.
9. Dryden, *Essays*, ed. Ker, II.1–2 (Dedication to *Examen Poeticum*).
10. Roger L'Estrange, *Citt and Bumpkin, in a Dialogue over a Pot of Ale* . . . (4th ed., 1680), pp. 2–3.
11. *The Intelligencer*, No. 1, 31 Aug. 1663.
12. Roger L'Estrange, *The Reformed Catholique* (2nd ed. "corrected," 1679), p. 5.
13. *The Intelligencer*, No. 1.
14. Daniel Defoe, *The Review*, I.[3–4] (The Preface).
15. Dryden, *Essays*, ed. Ker, I.253.
16. David Hume, *Essays Moral, Political and Literary*, ed. T. H. Green and T. H. Grose (1875), II.367.
17. J. Addington Symonds, *Essays Speculative and Suggestive* (1890), II.16.
18. For an excellent discussion of Johnson's prose, see W. K. Wimsatt, Jr., *The Prose Style of Samuel Johnson* (1941).
19. Samuel Johnson, *The Lives of the English Poets*, ed. G. B. Hill (1905), III.52.
20. Margaret Forbes, *Beattie and his Friends* (1904), p. 81.
21. Mark vi.39.
22. Laetitia-Matilda Hawkins, *Memoirs, Anecdotes, Facts and Opinions* (1824), I.73.

CHAPTER IV

1. *Jeffrey's Essays from 'The Edinburgh Review,'* "The New Universal Library" (n.d.), p. 289.
2. William Wordsworth, *The Prelude*, XIII.208–9.
3. *Edinburgh Review*, Aug. 1825.
4. Matthew Arnold, *Essays in Criticism*, First Series (1889), pp. 21ff.
5. *Ibid.*, pp. 23–24.
6. Matthew Arnold, *Essays in Criticism*, Second Series (1889), p. 44 ("The Study of Poetry").
7. Charles Dickens, *Our Mutual Friend*, ch. xi.
8. Thomas Hardy, *The Woodlanders*, ch. vii.
9. Leigh Hunt, *The Companion* (1828).
10. William Hazlitt, *Lectures on the English Comic Writers* (Everyman ed.), p. 39 (Lecture II: "On Shakespeare and Ben Jonson").
11. Thomas Carlyle, *Past and Present* (1888 ed.), p. 170 (Bk. III, ch. xi).
12. *Letters of Thomas Carlyle*, ed. Charles Eliot Norton (1889), pp. 497–99.
13. George Meredith, *The Egoist* (1879), I.105 (ch. vii).
14. *Ibid.*, I.187 ch. x).
15. *Ibid.*, I.152 (ch. ix).
16. John Addington Symonds, *In the Key of Blue and Other Prose Essays* (1893), p. 172.
17. Henry James, *A Small Boy and Others*, § 4.
18. *Times Literary Supplement*, 5 April, 1957.
19. *The Letters of D. H. Lawrence*, ed. Aldous Huxley (1932), pp. 232–33.
20. Virginia Woolf, *The Common Reader*, Second Series (1932), pp. 48–49.

INDEX

INDEX

122 INDEX